HARTMUT WILKE, PH.D.

My
Turtle

BARRON'S

CONTENTS

1 Getting to Know Turtles

2 The Way Turtles Want to Live

Welcome Home

Good Food Keeps a Turtle Fit and Healthy

5 Well Cared for and Healthy

6 Keeping Busy and Feeling Fine

Turtle Reproduction

7

What to Do When Problems Arise

8

Appendix

Getting to Know Turtles

A turtle's life is characterized by basking, looking for food, and some amazing "security techniques" that protect against enemies, drought, and cold.

230 Million Years of Turtle History

About 300 species of turtles are on Earth. Humans have paid tribute to them, ascribed mysterious powers to them, and simply eaten them. In the following pages, you can read how these creatures really live in the wild.

CAN YOU IMAGINE how long 170 million years ago is? That is when the first dinosaurs appeared on Earth. Sixty million years earlier, though, turtles were already present, witnessed the development of the dinosaurs and their demise, and have survived to this day! This means turtles have existed for 230 million years. The skeleton of a 3-foot-long (1 m) turtle that lived then is from a species in the genus *Proganochelys.* It has been found in both Thailand and Germany. Turtles have been able to withstand changing living conditions so far. Unfortunately, the healthy populations that existed just fifty years ago could be brought to the brink of extinction in only a few decades. This book thus deals with the proper ways to keep and handle turtles in the hope of contributing to their protection.

Turtles in Art, Mythology, and Medicine

Turtles have always fascinated people. They have inspired artistic representations, as ancient depictions in stone and ivory show. People try to imitate much of their behavior, such as constancy, wisdom, and composure.

Turtles have often been seen as immortal, fertile, and powerful. The whole creature, or parts of it, have been and are still used for treating numerous physical complaints. This use has not harmed turtles overall. In many areas of Earth, people consider turtles to be holy animals. In other areas, using turtles for medicinal purposes has usually been kept within ecologically justifiable bounds. The eating of turtles, whether as a delicacy for the wealthy or as a meal for the poor and hungry, has placed many species in danger. Other threats to turtles include the systematic collection from the wild

Shutters closed! ▶
Like other box turtles, the Mud Turtle *can close the opening in its bottom shell.*

to keep as pets and worldwide habitat destruction, forest degradation, and decreased availability of habitats.

What Turtles Are Like

In the course of their development on Earth, turtles have mastered both land and water and have split into numerous species and subspecies. This process is not over yet. The variety of species today occurs where there is plenty of sunshine, in the world's tropical and subtropical regions.

Some "emigrants" succeeded by adapting to the changeable climates in North America, Europe, and Australia. Turtles in these areas rest during the life-threatening heat, drought, or cold by either hibernating or estivating. North and South America are among the areas of the world richest in turtles; they are home to many species of swamp and mud turtles.

A Little Taxonomy

Among turtles there are differences between ocean, aquatic, and land turtles. Several species and subspecies

that form the latter two groups are presented in this book.

Ocean turtles spend their lives in the oceans and go onto land only to lay eggs. The Leatherback Turtle (*Dermatochelys coriacea*) is the largest living species of turtle on Earth, with a shell length of about 10 feet (3 m). It is also the only one that can raise its body temperature appreciably through muscle movement. As a result, the Leatherback can even visit the comparatively cold North Sea as an occasional guest.

Aquatic turtles live in all parts of the world in rivers and lakes, have mastered tropical mountain streams, and bury themselves in the mud of marshy ponds. Some species are good swimmers that rarely leave the water. Some species are poor swimmers that remain chiefly close to shore and "run around" under water. They are aquatic—living in the water. They include snake-necked turtles (Chelidae family), many swamp turtles (Emydidae family), and mud turtles (Kinosternidae family). The species that live primarily on the land are semiterrestrial (half on land), such as box and painted turtles. In any case, the eggs are laid on land, as with the ocean turtles.

Tortoises go as far as the steppes and deserts, where they meet their need for fluids by consuming plants with leaves that store water. They use the high humidity in holes (up to 80 percent) that also occur in deserts through rising (capillary) water. They are terrestrial—living on land.

A shell and armored legs constitute the traditional construction of a turtle.
▼

MATCHING TURTLES WITH THEIR HABITATS

WHAT THE BODY SHAPE TELLS US

	Land Dwelling (terrestrial)	Water Dwelling (aquatic)	Swamp Dwelling (amphibious)
Shell	Rounded arch	Shallow arch, like a rock polished on a streambed	All shapes from flat to rounded
Feet	Round, pillar shaped; thick, horny scales; thick, rather blunt claws	Paddle shaped with obvious webbing between toes, sharp claws	Paddle shaped, less-obvious or no webbing between toes, sharp claws
Behavior	Terrestrial, swims no more than an hour in shallow water, never dives	Seeks out water, stays in it, dives for several minutes to hours (depending on species)	Seeks out water, stays in it for hours and dives, also terrestrial (depending on species)

Turtles Are Loners

The various forms of turtles come equipped to handle their own individual survival. The solid shell of an adult turtle generally provides protection.

For young turtles, which can be easily swallowed whole or be carried off by birds, good protective coloration is the main defense that keeps them from being detected. Even some adult turtles are camouflaged, such as the Matamata (*Chelus fimbriatus*).

Aquatic turtles are the only ones that temporarily overlook their existence as loners, when a number of them climb onto the only tree trunk in the water to sun themselves. They do this only from a lack of basking places, though, and not to be sociable. One advantage in this is that one turtle will always have an eye peeled and can alarm the others by fleeing into the water if it spots a bird of prey. Then they all dive in, split up, and put an end to their "sociability."

The only intentional togetherness is generally restricted to the mating period. At that time, the males and females briefly get together to ensure the species' continued existence. Many encounters last only a few minutes. In other words, a turtle likes to live alone.

Physical Structure

Shell: This is the turtle's trademark. It consists of living bones from the spinal column, the ribs, and the shoulder blades as well as ossified portions of skin. As a part of the skeleton, it is involved in the growth process for a long time. The shell is covered by a periosteum. The shell forms protective horny plates on the outside that meet one another at the "seams." There the periosteum, which is sensitive to the touch, is exposed.

Many turtle shells have perceptible "growth rings" that provide information on the growth phases of the shell. However, they are not an indication of a turtle's age, like the growth rings in a tree.

With age, a tortoise's shell becomes somewhat bumpier and the horn plates thicken. As long as the turtle is healthy, entire horn plates will not come off. However, this is normal with many species of aquatic turtles, such as *Pseudemys, Chelodina,* and others. With age, the colors generally fade.

With many species, the shell becomes darker over time.

Limbs: The defense of most tortoises is completed by the thick horn and bone scales on the outside of the legs. When a tortoise enters its shell, it closes off the openings by turning the scaly sides of the limbs outward. All aquatic turtles possess only small, soft scales or none at all on their extremities; this increases their mobility.

Claws: All toes end in fairly long claws that grow continuously. In the wild, these claws are used in moving over rough ground. You should thus provide the turtle with some rough ground in the terrarium. If the claws are too long, the turtle can get caught in cracks and pull the nails out of the quick. Serious infections can result.

Beak: Another noteworthy characteristic is the creature's lack of teeth. The rim of the mouth, also referred to as the beak, is bordered by sharp horn edges that easily grind up plants and cut small creatures into pieces. In many tortoise species, the horn edges are serrated. As with a serrated knife, this makes it easier to split apart tough plant stems.

Perfectly Adapted to Their Habitat

Shell: In adapting to a great variety of habitats—depending on the species—the shell and its shape have undergone an extensive series of changes. Sea turtles, with their streamlined shell and paddle-shaped limbs, can reach speeds up to 43 mph (70 km/h), such as when they want to capture a speedy squid.

TIP

Claws for the courtship display

Long claws are not a development abnormality in all turtles. The males of North American Sliders have long claws on the front feet as secondary sex characteristics. With outstretched, trembling front legs, they entice the female during the courtship display.

The European Swamp Turtle *is an enthusiastic sun worshiper.* ▶

The very flat Pancake Tortoise (*Malacochersus tornieri*) from Africa has a shell that is so atrophied that it has become light and elastic like a fingernail. As a result, the limbs have more mobility. This, and its sharp claws, allows the turtle to climb high, even up vertical cliff walls.

The soft turtle is not protected by a bony shell but rather only a tough, elastic skin. In compensation, it has a powerful bite and spends most of its time well camouflaged and dug into soft bottoms below the water.

Still other species have developed a flap on their shell, which uses joints and hinges to close up the "house" completely when they pull in their head and limbs (see photo on p. 7).

Head: Aquatic turtles can be recognized by the shape of their head; the eyes and nose are located at the highest point. That way, the turtles can inconspicuously poke their eyes and nose out of the water when they are resting under the surface. They breathe and observe the surroundings without being detected by predators. The head and shell remain underwater, often concealed by floating material.

In contrast, a tortoise has to stretch its head much farther out of the water in order to breathe and see well at the same time since both the eyes and the opening for the nose are located lower on the head. Therefore, tortoises are generally more vulnerable to predators, such as birds of prey and various species of mammal.

A Turtle's Five Senses

Just like people, turtles have five senses. Searching for food, recognizing dangers, attracting a mate, and reproduction depend on these senses. Turtles see very well at a distance. They can recognize small objects even more than 30 feet (10 m) away. They react particularly to the colors yellow, red, and green and to movements. Good vision helps them search for food and a mate. Good vision also help them orient themselves in their surroundings when they need to find an appropriate hiding place or a sunny spot. Close in front of their eyes, these creatures do not see as clearly. With fairly poor vision, some species may be equipped to live in murky waters. They have

11

sharpened their other senses, such as smell and taste.

Hearing: A turtle's sense of hearing is comparatively weak and is geared toward low tones. Female turtles react to the male's guttural mating sound. In addition, the creatures can perceive vibrations on land and in the water through their shell. The sound waves are transmitted to the ear through the shell structure. The ear itself is covered by an external eardrum and skin. You can recognize it as a cross-shaped structure above the mandibular joint behind the eye.

Smell: In all turtles, the sense of smell is highly developed. They use their nose to find their food and a mate unerringly. Aquatic turtles pump the water back and forth through their nose by rhythmically expanding and contracting the roof of their mouth. Others let the tested water flow out through the mouth. Tortoises rhythmically move their throat (more precisely, their hyoid bone) when they want to deeply "breathe" a scent.

Taste: This sense is related to the sense of smell. Although the turtle's nose tests a food before consuming it, the food is once again submitted to a taste test inside the mouth.

Temperature sense: This is vital to survival. Temperature-sensing cells are located in the skin, especially in the front of the face and under the soles of the feet. They help the turtle identify reliable places that match its preferred temperature or are appropriate for laying eggs.

How Does a Turtle Breathe?

You have to look very closely if you want to see a turtle breathe because the shell does not move. Nearly everything takes place inside the shell, where muscles alternately expand and contract the lungs.

In deep breathing, the air exchange is supported with the rhythmic working of the front legs. A resting turtle needs nothing more for air transport than to raise and lower its throat, with support from the hyoid bone.

The lungs also serve aquatic turtles as swimming aids. They keep the creature horizontal and make it easier to dive by storing air with the help of special muscles. When the air is used up, the turtle must rise to the surface to breathe again.

◄ The Chinese Three-keeled Turtle
loves the warmth. When in temperate
latitudes, it is suited to an outdoor
life only in the peak of summer.

The "Solar Heating" Principle

Every turtle uses the solar heating principle because turtles cannot regulate their body temperature by themselves. Instead, they take on the temperature of their surroundings. If the temperature goes down, so does the turtle's body temperature. Animals with this type of dependency are referred to as cold-blooded.

Thanks to their temperature sense, turtles can seek places that are warm. Turtles can be seen in such places basking with limbs stretched out. They are often seen, for example, on logs in streams or on the banks of rivers. Even turtles that are active in the twilight bask in this manner in the sunrise and sunset.

Tortoises seek shade when their preferred temperature (depending on species, between 77° and 92°F/25° and 33°C) is exceeded. Aquatic turtles warm themselves in the top layer of water, which gets warmed by the sun, if that water is calm. To cool off, they dive into deeper, cooler water zones.

On land, dry embankments, gravel, and stones offer stored warmth for turtles even after the sun has ceased to shine. Thus, turtles can be seen huddling next to such features even after dark.

As a terrarium keeper, it is up to you to provide your turtle with the proper thermal environment. Your turtle must be able to warm and cool itself in the terrarium as necessary. This is very important to the turtle's well being, so don't overlook this aspect of the terrarium when you assemble it.

TEST

Are Turtles Right for Me?

Depending on the species, aquatic turtles and tortoises in the wild have a life expectancy of 60 to 100 years. Even in a terrarium, pet tortoises can reach the age of 60. So make certain that these animals are the right choice for you.

	Yes	No
1. An aquarium with a capacity of 55 to 110 gallons (200 to 400 L) can weigh 550 to 880 pounds (250 to 400 kg) with its base and technical accessories when the setup is filled with water. Can the structural engineering of your home take this, and is your landlord supportive?	○	○
2. Do you have a place in the yard for a pond or an outdoor pen with a hothouse so you can keep appropriate species there for the summer or attract food plants and animals?	○	○
3. During most of the year, even mating pairs are incompatible with one another. Do you have the space to set up a second aquarium or terrarium for the partner? Can you set up even a third one for raising the baby turtles?	○	○
4. Are you prepared to pay for the ongoing costs of electricity for the aquarium, food, and medical treatments?	○	○
5. Would you take a half-day's journey for good veterinary advice if you cannot find appropriate help in your area?	○	○

KEY: If you answered all five questions with "Yes," there are no further obstacles to your project. A single "No" is one reason to reconsider your intentions. If you answered with more than one "No," you should consider having a different pet in your home.

◀ *This Slider takes in plenty of sun on the surface of the water, which stores up lots of warmth and even lets through the ultraviolet rays.*

Behavior

Your turtle's behavior communicates its feelings and its needs: looking for concealment from predators, producing the optimal body temperature, avoiding excessive cold or heat, and finding a mate and an appropriate place to lay eggs. You will learn to tell if the turtle in your care is sick or in pain. During those times, its behavior will deviate from the norm. The more closely you observe and know your turtle, the sooner you will recognize behaviors that could indicate the need for veterinary treatment. Watching the varied behaviors of your turtle over the course of a year is also a highlight and a reward for your investment of time and money.

You should observe your turtle especially closely at the beginning. For example, if you see that it is fairly shy, you can help it acclimatize more easily by offering it more hiding places. You will likewise quickly determine if your aquatic turtle has problems in reaching the surface of the water and needs more underwater climbing opportunities. As you study your turtle, you will also notice whether or not it can easily use its basking place.

Below is outlined the behavior of a healthy, well-acclimated turtle. Whether you have a tortoise or an aquatic turtle, you should be able to recognize the described behaviors.

A Day in the Life of a Turtle

Species active during the day: After a night's rest, an adult turtle seeks a place where it can absorb and store up warmth in order to reach its preferred temperature of 77° to 92°F (25° to 33°C).

In most cases, this is accomplished by sunbathing. If the enclosure is large enough, the turtle attentively looks around, calmly eats its food, and looks for more treats. Then it pulls back to take a rest and digest. If necessary, it will bask some more because a good body temperature is important for well-regulated digestion.

At midday, the turtle again looks for food and then takes another rest. After that, it withdraws into its hiding place for the night. The daily routine is similar for young turtles, but they stay in the open only a short time while they look for food.

Species active at twilight: In the half-light of dawn, the turtle first seeks food and then takes in the warmth of the early-morning sun. After that, it retreats to its hiding place for the hours of morning and afternoon sunlight. After dusk in the evening, it again looks for food and then rests for the remainder of the night in its hiding place. It follows the same unchanging routine day after day throughout its entire lifetime.

Mating Time

Mating partners recognize each other by scent across several yards, without even having to see one another. This is true for both tortoises and especially for aquatic turtles.

If you are keeping a mating pair of tortoises in a divided area, you will recognize this behavior by the fact that the creatures try to get over the wall that is keeping them apart.

When you put the creatures together, the male begins to court the female. Depending on the species, this can be very charming (as with Painted Turtles and Sliders, creatures from the

MY PET

Do you know your turtle's daily routine?

For this test, the enclosure or aquarium must be exposed to natural daylight or else the lighting must imitate the timing of daylight. Artificial light should thus be no longer or shorter in duration than the length of the day.

The test begins:

Cover the viewing side of the enclosure with a sheet of wrapping paper so the turtle cannot see you. That way you will avoid the conditioning effect ("Ah, I'm going to get some food!"). Small peepholes allow you to watch the turtle surreptitiously. In the course of twenty-four hours, note when the creature is active and when it rests. Now you know precisely when to feed and when to leave it in peace.

My test results:

Emydura genus), or very direct, without any courtship to speak of (musk turtles).

Male tortoises go around the female and get it to stand still by ramming the shell or gently biting its front legs. If the female is ready, she remains motionless with head and front legs drawn in—and the mating occurs without injury.

into their darkest hiding place. They may come out again, but they will not eat anything more. Eventually, they enter hibernation.

When the temperatures in the spring begin to climb, the turtles will become lively again on their own. Tortoises take a long bath, drink, and

If you write down your observations, the result is an **interesting diary**. It will serve as a calendar for recurring events.

Some weeks later, the female uses its hind legs to scrape out a hollow on the land in which to deposit the eggs. Then it completely covers the eggs with dirt. Before laying the eggs, the turtle becomes temporarily aggressive toward other turtles in the same pen.

The Rhythm of a Year

If the summer is very hot, many species of turtle hide or bury themselves, possibly for several weeks of summer rest. These include the Russian Tortoise and the Williams Mud Turtle. The latter estivate when the water in which they live dries up. The animals do not want to be disturbed during their summer rest phase; they will wake up on their own at the appropriate time.

Turtles that hibernate completely empty their intestine in the fall (October and November) and crawl

begin taking in food after about a week.

Note: Tropical species do not hibernate.

Recognizing Behavior as an Alarm Signal

Deviations from normal behavior are an alarm signal. Here are the two most common ones:

▸ Your turtle still is not eating two or three weeks after hibernation, possibly losing weight, and spends the whole day under the spotlight or in the water tank. Evidently, it became sick during hibernation. Take the turtle to the veterinarian.

▸ A lack of appetite other than during estivation and hibernation can be due to either bad weather or a low temperature. If the appetite does not return when the weather improves, your turtle needs to go to the veterinarian.

◀ **1** **Floating plants** make this Yellow-cheeked Slider invisible from above. At the same time, it can get air under the plant cover without having to betray its hiding place.

Roots and stones serve as resting places under water for mediocre swimmers such as the Caspian Stream Turtle. These types of climbing aids are important in helping turtles get air comfortably. **2** ▶

◀ **3** **Decorative stones** in the outdoor pen serve a tortoise by providing shade, storing up warmth, creating obstacles for athletic exercises, and keeping the claws worn down.

A digging area with soft, moist dirt is an important accessory in the pen for every tortoise so it can dig in if need be. **4** ▶

Lifestyle

The type of food greatly determines the lifestyle and the size of the territory (enclosure size, need for space). This becomes especially clear when you take a closer look at how the turtle gets its food.

Active hunters: These include young Painted Turtles and Sliders plus Yellow-turtles as the Matamata and the Soft Shell.

"Grazers:" Figuratively speaking, this name can be applied to omnivores such as adult Painted Turtles and Sliders. They search about and "graze" on small creatures on plant stems and the ground. Even tortoises can be "grazers." They ingest vegetation and grasses they find while wandering.

Attention: In the wild, turtles also occasionally eat a few morsels of soil. If this happens, it is part of your turtle's

DID YOU KNOW THAT . . .

. . . turtles can die from stress?

The mere sight of a dominant animal that they cannot get away from can lead to apathy and death in turtles. The example of a Matamata confirms this. A mating pair of this species was put into a pen together. As a result, one of the animals stopped eating—evidently it was stressed. The turtle was put into the neighboring aquarium, where it could still see the dominant animal through the glass. Since it never resumed eating, the turtle died within a couple of months, before the owners had figured out the problem. The animal lay motionless on the ground and appeared only to lack appetite. An autopsy revealed no organic disease. The conclusion was that the Matamata had died of stress. Nobody had realized how much stress the dominant animal could cause through a mere glance.

margined Box Turtles and *Terrapene* species. They pursue their prey purposefully, even when it runs away (crickets, millipedes).

Lurkers: They camouflage themselves underwater to become invisible—and remain motionless until the prey comes into reach. Patient lurkers include such nature and harmless. Just be sure the specifications for the soil indicated in this handbook have been observed. If your turtle keeps taking in fairly large amounts of dirt, it is lacking something. Usually the turtle needs minerals. Take the turtle to the vet. Check the food to see if it supplies a good amount of calcium and the right balance of calcium and phosphorus.

Body Language

You can tell immediately how people you know are feeling, depending on whether they are hanging their head or in a good mood.

At first, doing this will be difficult with the turtle. If you observe your turtle carefully, over time you will soon be able to evaluate correctly how it feels. Here are the most important behavior patterns and what they mean.

Basking: A healthy turtle likes to lie under the heat lamp or in the sunlight. It extends its head and legs far out to catch as many rays as possible.

Good: The turtle basks for hours several times a day.

Questionable: It lies under the heat source all day long without taking a break. The turtle may be sick, or the heat source may be too weak. (Check the heat source again.)

Water bathing: A tortoise (excluding a Russian Tortoise) lies in its pool of water. It may drink or empty its intestine.

Good: It appears alert and leaves the water after 5 to 20 minutes.

Questionable: It spends several hours lying in the water, lets its head droop, and appears listless and tired. The cause for this behavior may be some illness. Play it safe and have the turtle examined by a vet.

Digging hollows: Sexually mature females dig hollows with their hind feet, preferably near a heat lamp, or in dirt hillocks in the outdoor pen. This usually happens in the late evening hours.

Good: After digging hollows, the turtle lays eggs and covers them up with dirt.

Questionable: The turtle lays no eggs, remains restless, and may dig further hollows. There is a danger of egg binding. Take your turtle to the veterinarian.

"Pumping" with the front legs: The turtle stands on all fours and rhythmically pulls in the front legs— what is technically known as "pumping."

Good: This is a temporary phenomenon after an exertion that deepens the breathing.

Questionable: If the pumping occurs constantly, and is possibly associated with breathing noises, the turtle must be brought to the vet. Some illness may be the cause.

The Yellow-cheeked Slider *attentively gazes at its surroundings.*
▼

Digging in the dirt: The turtle digs horizontally into the dirt a third to a half of its length. The head and part of the shell stick out.

Good: Species that are active in the twilight spend the day resting in this position.

Questionable: Turtles that are active during the day may find it too warm or too dry inside the terrarium. You should check the living conditions.

Mating behavior with stones: Males mount stones that resemble the shape of a turtle shell. This is not a cause for concern. It is only what's known as displacement behavior in a sexually active male that has no access to a female.

Young tortoises—Greek in this instance—live a life of concealment in their early years. They could be too easy for crows to find.

▼

Turtle Species

The agony of deciding: If you have little or no experience in owning turtles, I recommend species that are easy or very easy to raise. Meeting the vital needs of these species is relatively easy.

THE FOLLOWING PAGES present 26 species, including a fairly complete profile of 16 of them. All of these species meet the following criteria:

▶ Many of them remain so small that they can be kept in an indoor setup all year long, in case you do not have an outdoor pen for your pet.

▶ They are bred in captivity (see breeding statistics that are available online), so generally they are easy to find in pet shops.

▶ From the profiles, you can determine which species need an aquarium, an aqua-terrarium, or a terrarium and whether or not the species needs a rest in the winter or summer.

▶ Note the specifications on the size of the setups; they take into account the animals' behavior, for some species need larger enclosures.

Chart: Pages 30 and 31 list 10 more species that, because of their particular demands for care, caging, nutrition, and reproduction, can be recommended only to owners with a bit more experience.

Notice: Very large, heavy species and others that are considered fussy have not been included—even if they are available in pet shops because they are appropriate for experienced enthusiasts. The space requirements of larger species are also particularly great. They need

terrariums the size of a room and out-door pens of about a hundred square yards. For these reasons, you will find no information about the following species:

Common Snapping Turtle (*Chelydra serpentine*), up to 18½ inches (47 cm), 48 pounds (22 kg); Yellow-footed Tortoise (*Geochelone denticulata*), up to 24 inches (60 cm), highest weight unknown; African Spurred Tortoise (*Geochelone sulcata*), 31½ inches (80 cm), up to 132 pounds (60 kg); Alligator Snapping Turtle (*Macroclemys temmincki*), 27½ inches (70 cm), up to 220 pounds (100 kg); Florida Peninsula Cooter (*Pseudemys floridana*), Eastern River Cooter (*P. concinna*), and Florida Red-bellied Cooter (*P. nelsoni*), the females of which can grow as large as 16 inches (40 cm).

TIP

Mixed breeds

A mixed-breed turtle comes from mating different species or subspecies. Many times, a lay person will not even recognize one. When the distribution areas of two species overlap, mongrels can occur even in the wild. Most frequently, though, they result from people breeding different species. Mongrels should not be used for breeding purposes for reasons of species protection.

Active during the day, lives aquatically in open water; does not hibernate; protein diet. Average adult size around 7 inches (18 cm). Animals of Australian origin reach 10 inches (25 cm). Best reproduction rates in captivity.

Red-bellied Short-necked Turtle
Emydura subglobosa

Two subspecies (depending on author): *E. s. subglobosa* and *E. s. worrellii*. **Distribution:** Southern New Guinea as far as the adjacent northern tip of Australia (Cape York, Jardine River and tributaries). Inhabits large running and still waters. **Living conditions:** Year-round in an aquarium (at least 80 gallons/300 L total volume for one to two animals), water depth at least 16 inches (40 cm). Water temperature 77°F (25°C) from November through February, 81°F (27°C) for the rest of the year. Daytime air temperature 2°F (1°C) higher than the water temperature. Provide UV and daylight if the turtle spends all its time in the aquarium. The turtle may also bask in the water. If this happens, double the UV illumination time. Can be kept outdoors only during the heat of midsummer and in a location sheltered from the wind. **Behavior:** Swims very well, rarely comes onto land, sometimes shy. **Special concerns:** Interesting courtship display (ritual fanning with the front legs and nodding the head). Eggs are laid from April through June with about 7 to 10 eggs per clutch; multiple clutches are possible in a year. Hatching after 6 or 7 weeks at 82°F (28°C). Side-neck.

Active during the day; lives aquatically on the shore; hibernates (depending on origin); protein diet. Average adult size around 7 inches (17 cm), rarely 8 inches (20 cm). Very good reproduction rate in captivity.

European Pond Turtle
Emys orbicularis

Thirteen subspecies, including *E. o. orbicularis* (Central Europe), *E. o. hellenica* (Po plains, Balkans), *E. o. fritzjuergenobsti* (Spain). **Distribution:** Central and southern Europe, the Balkans, Northwest Africa. **Living conditions:** Can be kept year-round in an aqua-terrarium. The water portion requires a minimal surface area of 20 × 48 inches (120 × 50 cm) and a depth of 16 inches (40 cm). Water temperature 72° to 77°F (22° to 25°C), with additional spotlights. Provide UV and daylight if turtle spends all its time in the aquarium; a better option is complementary time in an outdoor pen. For mating pairs, use two small ponds that can be separated rather than one. **Behavior:** Good swimmer; likes to bask on land; sometimes shy. **Special concerns:** With age, takes in very little plant food (10%). Aside from the mating season, females must be separated from males. Eggs are laid starting around June, usually in the evening. Clutch of 12 or more eggs buried about 2 inches (10 cm) deep. Hatching after about three months. If you get young turtles bred in captivity, get a pure subspecies. **Similar care requirements:** Species of river and stream turtles from the *Mauremys spp.* genus. Few offspring in captivity.

Painted Turtle
Chrysemis picta

Four subspecies, the smallest is *C. picta dorsalis*, the Southern Painted Turtle. The subspecies also form mixed breeds in the wild. **Distribution:** Southern Canada to the American Gulf Coast. In addition to the South, widely distributed toward the West. **Living conditions:** Aquarium 20 × 48 inches (50 × 120 cm) and preferably water deeper than 16 inches (40 cm) (= 66 gallons/ 240 L). For larger species, 83 gallons (300 L). Water temperature 73° to 81°F (23° to 27°C), depending on origin. If turtle is kept exclusively in aquarium, provide UV and daylight with strong spotlights; basking place at 104°F (40°C) on the land portion (spotlight). Additional outdoor time recommended. Turtle must usually be kept alone in an aquarium because of incompatibility. **Behavior:** Good swimmer; likes to bask on land; usually aggressive toward fellow occupants, especially in close living quarters. **Special concerns:** Both females and males (especially) are very incompatible. Females from *C. p. dorsalis* are sexually mature around age 2. Eggs are laid from around May to July in 1 to 3 clutches with 1 to 14 eggs each. The smaller species produces the smaller clutches. Hatching after about 2 months.

Active during the day; lives aquatically in open water; hibernates at 41°F (5°C); mixed diet. Average adult size: males up to 4½ inches (11 cm), females around 6 inches (15 cm). Good reproduction rate in captivity.

Common Musk Turtle / Stinkpot
Sternotherus odoratus

No subspecies. **Distribution:** From southeastern Canada through the eastern U.S. down to Florida. On soft-bottomed standing or slow-running waters. **Living conditions:** Aquaterrarium, 40 inches (100 cm) long, 16 inches (40 cm) wide, and 20 inches (50 cm) high (= 55 gallons/200 L); water depth 10 to 12 inches (25 to 30 cm) for adults (= about 43 gallons/ 100 L of water) and 4 to 6 inches (10 to 15 cm) for young turtles. Water temperature 77°F (25°C). Provide access to daylight, warming and UV bath under water, sandy bottom about 1 inch (2 cm) thick. Put climbing aids into the water, plus some dark hiding places (cork tubes) with easy access to the surface. **Behavior:** Rarely basks in top layer of water; also active at dawn and dusk; spends the day in a hiding place. Rarely swims; walks and climbs much more on roots and stones. Not frequently on land but may venture forth to take in food. **Special concerns:** Best kept alone, including mating pairs outside the mating season. Clutch of 2 to 4 eggs. After 11 or 12 weeks, the young turtles hatch out, no larger than beetles.

Nocturnal, lives in water (aquatic) near the shore; turtles of northern origin hibernate: 2 to 3 months at 41° to 50°F (5° to 20°C) on land; protein diet. Average adult size: males, 4 inches (10 cm); females, 3½ inches (9 cm). Good reproduction rate in captivity.

Active during the day, lives in water and on land; depending on origin, 3 months hibernation at 39° to 45°F (4° to 7°C) in the water; otherwise active at 55° to 59°F (13° to 15°C) but then eats less; protein diet, in older age 10% plant diet. Male up to 5 inches (12 cm), females up to 7 inches (18 cm). Good offspring in captivity.

Reeve's Turtle or Chinese Three-keeled Pond Turtle

Chinemys reevesii

Two subspecies: *C. r. reevesii*, *C. r. megalocephala*, around 30 local variants. **Distribution:** Southeast China, Taiwan, Japan, Hong Kong. Shallow water, moist areas. **Living conditions:** Aqua-terrarium, 48 inches (120 cm) long, 24 inches (60 cm) wide, and 20 inches (50 cm) high (= about 100 gallons/360 L). Water depth around 8 inches (20 cm) for grown turtles (= 16½ gallons/60 L), 2 to 3 inches (5 to 7 cm) (= about 5 gallons/18 L) for young turtles. Water temperature, 75° to 79°F (24° to 26°C), plus a spotlight at 104°F (40°C); ask the breeder about preferred temperature or find out by testing. Land portion with narrow openings (pine roots, turf). Basking place in a corner of the land portion with UV and daylight supply. Outdoor living recommended. **Behavior:** Poor swimmer; young turtles preferably in water, older ones also on land. Young and old sun themselves on land. Peaceable toward other turtles of all species facilitates living with other turtles (not for beginners) and reproduction. **Special concerns:** Males from age 6 and up often melanistic (black). Clutch of 2 to 8 eggs generally in June; several clutches per year possible. The 1 inch (3 cm) young hatch after 8 to 10 weeks.

Active during the day, lives amphibiously near the shore; hibernation in the water; depending on origin, 2 to 3 months at 45°F (7°C) or 6 to 7 months at 37° to 39°F (3° to 4°C); protein diet; adults need 10% plant diet. Final size around 4 inches (10 cm). Few offspring in captivity.

Spotted Turtle

Clemmys guttata

No subspecies. **Distribution:** Southeastern Canada to Florida, in the eastern U.S.; swamps, calm waters, marsh waters. **Living conditions:** Aqua-terrarium, 3 feet (1 m) long, 16 inches (40 cm) wide, 20 inches (50 cm) high (= 55 gallons/200 L); always very clean water, just 2 inches (5 cm) deep for young turtles (= 5½ gallons/20 L of water) and 8 inches (20 cm) deep (= 22 gallons/ 80 L) for adult turtles. Preferred water temperature depends on origin, in the 72° to 81°F (22° to 27°C) range; ask the breeder or test; plus spotlight at 104°F (40°C). Starting at around 3 inches (8 cm), increase land portion to 16 × 20 inches (50 × 40 cm). Access to UV and daylight; backyard pond in the summer. **Behavior:** Must be kept singly since even females are incompatible with one another. If the water is too cold for the turtles, they sun themselves a lot on grass clumps or dry stumps. **Special concerns:** Mating in water only under supervision, then immediately separate the turtles. Two to 8 eggs starting in May, 2 to 3 clutches per year possible. Hatching after around 2 months. In the wild, females are sexually mature only at age of 7 through 15, males at 7 to 13. Greatest age in females up to 110 years (only in the most northern distribution areas), males up to 65.

Striped Mud Turtle
Kinosternon baurii

Two subspecies: *K. b. palmarum, K. b. bauri.* **Distribution:** Florida, South Georgia. Swamps and calm waters, soft bottom. **Living conditions:** Aquarium, 3 feet (1 m) long, 16 inches (40 cm) wide, and 20 inches (50 cm) high (= 55 gallons/200 L), water depth 2 inches (5 cm) for young turtles (= 5 gallons/20 L); 12 inches (30 cm) for adults (= about 33 gallons/120 L); 1 inch (2 cm) of fine sand on the bottom. Preferred water temperature according to area of origin, 64° to 82°F (18° to 28°C); ask the breeder or test. Put in thread algae, egeria, and mouse-eared chickweed for cover. Provide hiding places with foam peanuts up to 1½ inches (3 cm) on a side as a substitute for decayed plant matter. Tree stump/sunning island in the middle of the water. Access to UV and daylight. Put in roots or a sisal rope (1½ inches/4 cm in diameter) underwater. **Behavior:** Somewhat shy; climbs underwater, also swims. Peaceable, even as mating pair. If males are persistent, they must be separated from the females. **Special concerns:** Two hinges on lower shell. Males have horny spike on end of tail and patches of rough scales on hind legs. Sexually mature at age 5 to 7. One to 8 eggs in the spring, 1 to 3 clutches per year possible. Hatching after 3 to 5 months.

Active during the day, in the water close to shore; possible hibernation, depending on origin: 3 to 4 months at 45° to 55°F (7° to 13°C) in bed of decayed plant matter; check behavior for tendency. Summer rest possible. Mixed diet (75% protein). Ultimate size: males, 3½ inches (9 cm), females 4¾ inches (12 cm). Few offspring.

Common Snake-necked Turtle
Chelodina longicollis

No subspecies. **Distribution:** Eastern Australia; swamps, calm waters. **Living conditions:** Aquarium, 48 inches (120 cm) long, 20 inches (50 cm) wide; 16 to 20 inches (40 to 50 cm) of water (= 58 to 83 gallons/240 to 300 L) is adequate for two females. Keep males in separate tanks with a total capacity of 55 gallons (200 L) each. Water temperature 72° to 81°F (22° to 27°C). Provide UV and daylight, spotlight at 104°F (40°C) shining on land portion, ramp, or water (test for preference); will be rarely used. Backyard pond in peak summer recommended. **Behavior:** Lively swimmer that enjoys hunting live food in the water (crickets, and so on). Generally only the females climb onto the land to bask and lay eggs. During the mating season, the otherwise peaceable creatures become temporarily snappy. **Special concerns:** "Side-necked" turtle that protects its head and long neck by tucking it to the side between top and bottom shells. Large clutch of 8 to 18 eggs; hatching after 8 to 10 weeks. I attribute my own breeding success to high-quality nutrition from whole, freshly killed fish (guppies) and newborn mice (frozen, from pet shops).

Active during the day, lives in the water close to shore; possible hibernation from December through February at a water temperature of 59° to 61°F (15° to 16°C) and with little food; test; protein diet (live food). Ultimate size, males: 7½ inches; females: 8 inches (20 cm). Reproduction infrequent.

Active in half-light, a swamp turtle that prefers to live on land; hibernates; mixed diet, young turtles get a higher percentage of protein (80%) in the first year or two. Average ultimate size, 4 to 8 inches (10 to 20 cm), depending on subspecies; few offspring in captivity; steer clear of mixed breeds.

Eastern Box Turtle
Terrapene carolina

Six subspecies: *T. c. carolina, T. c. major, T. c. triunguis* in shops; the others are essentially unavailable. **Distribution:** U.S., except in the West. Moist forest areas and meadows. **Living conditions:** Terrarium with at least 13 sqare feet (1.2 sq m) surface area and outdoor enclosure with heated hothouse. Very important: one-fourth of the enclosure at 97°F (36°C) (spotlight at 113°F/45°C), otherwise air temperature 68°F (20°C) at night to 82°F (28°C) during the day; ground temperature 68° to 79°F (20° to 26°C). Adapt the environment in the terrarium and the hothouse to the subspecies. Sensitive to excessively cool conditions (be careful outdoors). Except for *T. c. triunguis*, all subspecies are sensitive to dry air (i.e., below 70% humidity). Bathing tank 2 to 3 inches (6 to 8 cm) deep. Access to UV and daylight. **Behavior:** Likes morning and evening sun, lies in the water for hours. In dry periods, digs in for weeks at a time. **Special concerns:** At ages 2 to 6, has movable joints on lower shell. *T. c. carolina* only 6½ inches (16 cm), *T. c. major* grows to a maximum of 8 inches (20 cm), swims well and lives near water. In contrast, *T. c. triunguis* prefers a drier environment. Clutch of 1 to 8 eggs, hatching after 2 months.

Active during the day, lives amphibiously, mostly in the water; depending on subspecies, 2 to 4 months hibernation at 64°F (18°C) (on land portion with no heating); primarily plant diet. Size around 8 inches (20 cm), still few offspring in captivity.

Amboina Box Turtle or Southeast Asian Box Turtle
Cuora amboinensis

Four subspecies: *C. a. kamaroma*, commonly kept as a pet; *C. a. amboinensis, C. a. cuoro, C. a. lineate*. **Distribution:** In Southeast Asia from Myanmar to the Philippines and Indonesia. Shallow, slow-moving waters, soft ground. **Living conditions:** Can be kept in aqua-terrarium year-round, water portion with sandy bottom 48 × 20 inches (120 × 50 cm) surface area and 8 inches (20 cm) high (= 33 gallons/120 L). Water 77° to 81°F (25° to 27°C), air 82° to 86°F (28° to 30°C), plus spotlight at 104°F (40°C). Climbing aids in fairly dark water region with lots of cover. Access to UV and daylight on land; roomy land portion in case the turtle prefers to use it. Outdoor living in peak summer. **Behavior:** Males are tireless, often aggressive suitors (keep them separated); female often territorial (keep singly). In very roomy outdoor enclosures, several females may be kept together. **Special concerns:** Depending on origin, a turtle may prefer living on land (observe and adjust the terrarium accordingly). Several clutches per year, each with 1 to 5 eggs. Hatching after 8 to 9 weeks; young turtles raised in shallow water. Subspecies mixed breeds are available in shops. Look for pure strains.

Active in the day; hibernation 3 months if living in hothouse, otherwise 5 months. Plant diet. Average ultimate size up to 10 inches (25 cm). Very good breeding results.

Boettger's Tortoise or Eastern Hermann's Tortoise

Testudo hermanni boettgeri

Distribution: Greece, Turkey, Romania, Bulgaria, Albania, Serbia, and Croatia. Overgrown meadows, shady, bushy landscapes. The territory contains areas of water. **Living conditions:** Terrarium at least 13 square feet (1.2 sq m); must be kept outdoors in the summer and preferably all year long if a hothouse is available. Ground temperature 68 to 73°F (20° to 23°C), air temperature 64° to 70°F (18° to 26°C). Also spotlight at 104°F (40°C). Provide thick cover for young tortoises, and secure outdoor enclosure against birds of prey with a protective net. **Behavior:** Active in early morning and late afternoon. Likes to climb and dig; with proper care and adequate space, lively and fond of exercise. **Special concerns:** Characteristics include a pronounced horn spike at the end of the tail and (usually) a divided tail carapace. Mixed breeds involving Boettger's and Mediterranean Spur Thigh occur. Not suitable for purebred breeding. Females become sexually mature at around 10 to 14 years, males at 5 to 7. Clutch with 3 to 8 eggs starting in the spring, up to 3 clutches per year. Hatching after 2 to 3 months.

Active during the day; 3 months of hibernation in hothouse, otherwise about 5 months; herbivorous. Ultimate size around 12 inches (30 cm); maximum size up to about 14 inches (35 cm). Very good breeding results.

Marginated Tortoise

Testudo marginata

Two subspecies, depending on author: *T. m. marginata, T. m. weissingeri.* **Distribution:** Greece, southern peninsula; preferably on karstic slopes in dry areas ("maquis"). **Living conditions:** In terrarium at least 13 square feet (1.2 sq m); needs to be kept outdoors in summer and preferaby year-round if a hothouse is available. Ground temperature 68° to 73°F (20° to 23°C), air temperature 64°F (18°C) at night, up to 81°F (27°C) during the day. Also spotlight at 113°F (45C°). Cover for young tortoises. **Behavior:** Active in early morning and late afternoon. Likes to climb and dig; with proper care and sufficient space, lively and fond of exercise. Lives less in hiding than the Boettger's Tortoise and also does not avoid direct sunlight. **Special concerns:** Largest European tortoise. Males' top shell with curved rear edge gives the tortoise its name. Two clutches possible per year, with 3 to 8 eggs. Hatching after 2 to 3 months. Mixed breeds between Marginated Tortoise and Mediterranean Spur Thigh Tortoise (in both the wild and in captivity). Avoid for breeding purposes.

Active during the day; hibernation in the wild 6 to 7 months, additional summer rest possible; primarily herbivorous. Ultimate size, 10 to 12 inches (25 to 30 cm). Good breeding results.

Mediterranean Spur Thigh Tortoise
Testudo graeca

Approximately 6 subspecies. Mediterranean Spur Thigh Tortoise, *T. g. graeca* North Africa, Southern Spain, the Balearic Islands, and Sardinia; with *T. (g.) soussensis* (southern Morocco) further uncertain subspecies; Eurasian Tortoise, *T. g. ibera* (southeastern Europe), *T. g. terrestris* (southeastern Asia Minor), *T. g. armeniaca* (Armenia, Turkey), *T. g. buxtoni* (Eastern Caucasus-Iran), *T. g. zarudnyi* (eastern Iran). **Distribution:** See subspecies. Steppes, brushy land, dry forests, semiarid deserts, cultivated land. **Living conditions:** Terrarium at least 13 square feet (1.2 sq m); outdoor living required in summer and preferably year-round if a hothouse is available. Ground temperature from 72° to 77°F (22° to 25°C), air temperature 68°F (20°C) at night and up to 82°F (28°C) during the day. Also a spotlight at 104°F (40°C). Likes the warmth. **Behavior:** Lively, good digger. **Special concerns:** Horned cone next to thigh. Plant diet rich in protein in the spring, animal protein (5% insects, snails) for fiber-rich diet from summer on. For animals with origin outside of Europe, climate and nutrition can be provided only with care and lots of effort. One to 3 clutches of eggs per year with 4 to 8 eggs each. Hatching after 2 to more than 3 months.

Active during the day; generally rests in the summer and always hibernates; herbivorous. Average ultimate size around 8 inches (20 cm). Average breeding results.

Russian Tortoise
Testudo [Agrionemys] horsfieldii

Three subspecies, depending on author: *T. h. horsfieldii, T. h. kazakhstanica, T. h. rustamovi.* **Distribution:** East of the Caspian Sea, Iran to Pakistan. Dry, open, karstic steppes; rocks, sand, and loam. **Living conditions:** terrarium at least 13 square feet (1.2 sq m) for young animals (fall, spring) and outdoor living in the summer; outdoor living year-round if a hothouse is available. Ground temperature from 68° to 73°F (20° to 23°C), air temperature 64°F (18°C) at night, up to 79°F (26°C) during the day. Also, spotlight at 104°F (40°C). Cover for young animals. **Behavior:** Active in the early morning and later afternoon. Good climber; digs long passageways. With proper care and good plant availability, lively and fond of exercise. **Special concerns:** In the wild, active for only 3 months of the year (March through May). Summer rest can transition into hibernation without a break (6 to 7 months). Then the animal immediately needs high temperatures and dry living conditions. Cold, dry summers are very bad for health. A healthy animal never goes into the water. Sexually mature males are aggressive; they need to be kept singly. Reproduction as with the Boettger's Tortoise.

Red-footed Tortoise
Geochelone carbonaria

No subspecies; broad geographical distribution produces a variety of body and head sizes as well as head and skin colorations. **Distribution:** Panama to Argentina in the tropical rain forest or in subtropical savannas. **Living conditions:** Terrarium 15 to 25 square feet (1.5 to 2.5 sq m) only for raising young animals. Growing animals kept in a room (at least 100 square feet/10 sq m) or greenhouse (at least 80 square feet/8 sq m) with heating and sprinkler setup; in addition, outdoor enclosure (at least 300 square feet/30 sq m) with shade plants. Special climatic demands: ground temperature 72°F (22°C) at night, up to 77°F (25°C) during the day, air temperature 77°F (24°C) at night, up to 90°F (32°C) during the day. Air humidity 80% to 90% year-round. HQI-TS spotlight (bright light) along with a spotlight (104°F/40°C) to avoid reduction in temperature, especially in the winter. Create tropical "dry season" in winter in temperate latitudes by suspending use of the sprinkler. Swimming tank at 75° to 81°F (24° to 27°C), 6 inches (15 cm) of water. **Behavior:** Very fond of exercise. **Special concerns:** Plant food rich in fiber and juice. Very pronounced need for space and for climate control. Three to 4 clutches per year with 4 to 5 eggs possible; hatching after 4 to 5 months.

Active during the day; no hibernation; mixed diet (plants, plus small portions of protein from insects every 2 to 3 weeks). Average ultimate size around 14 inches (35 cm), 20 inches (50 cm) also possible. Regular reproduction in captivity.

Pancake Tortoise
Malacochersus tornieri

No subspecies. **Distribution:** Chiefly Kenya and Tanzania in isolated rocky formations (kopjes), hiding places in deep rock fissures. **Living conditions:** terrarium at least 15 square feet (1.5 sq m), ground temperature 65°F (18°C) at night, up to 79°F (26°C) during the day, plus spotlight at 104°F (40°C). Access to UV and daylight. All-day air temperature to be selected in the 77° to 86°F (23° to 30°C) range. Rock fissures (hiding place made from layered rock slabs). Temperature there 64°F (18°C) at night, up to 72°F (22°C) during the day. Make the fissures tighter at the bottom and keep them moist for the tortoise to slip into. Lots of space in front of the "rock formation"; firm, dry loam bottom for the run. **Behavior:** Very good climber, active only for a few hours a day. **Special concerns:** Flexible shell; when the legs are drawn in, it swells and can wedge in the rock. Males have a spur between the tail and the hind legs. Difficult to keep outdoors because summer in a temperate climate is like the African winter. Often peaceable as long as an adequate number of hiding places are available. Each year 2 to 3 rather elongated eggs are laid singly about 6 to 8 weeks apart. Hatching after 5 to 8 months.

Active during the day (morning, evening); no hibernation, but a few weeks of summer rest possible; herbivorous. Average ultimate size 6 to 8 inches (15 to 20 cm), reproduction rare in temperate latitudes; only for experienced owners.

MORE TURTLE SPECIES WITH SPECIAL REQUIREMENTS

Species	Average Ultimate Size Male/Female	Indoor/Outdoor Enclosure (surface area)
Chelus fimbriatus **Matamata**	14/16 in. (35/40 cm) Very few offspring in captivity	Aquarium, 55 gal. (200 L), shallow water, dusky, shallow sandy shore, avoid sight of neighboring animals
Cuora flavomarginata **Yellow-Margined Box Turtle**	8/8 in. (20/20 cm) Very few offspring in captivity	Terrarium, 9 sq. ft. (0.9 sq m), at least 70% air humidity, with shallow water portion
Geochelone elegans **Indian Star Tortoise**	8/14 in. (20/36 cm) Very few offspring in captivity	Large terrarium at least 150 sq. ft. (15 sq m) and outdoor living indispensable
Geochelone pardalis **Leopard Tortoise**	18/20 in. (35/50 cm) Few offspring in captivity	Large terrarium at least 200 sq. ft. (20 sq m.) for a mating pair; outdoor living indispensable
Geomyda spengleri **Vietnamese or Black-breasted Leaf Turtle**	4½/4¾ in. (11/12 cm) Few offspring in captivity	Aqua-terrarium over 3 ft. (1 m) long, water portion and hiding places, dimly lighted
Indotestudo elongata **Elongated or Yellow-headed Tortoise**	12/12 in. (20/20 cm) Offspring in captivity fairly common	Terrarium at least 150 sq. ft. (15 sq m), dim, climate according to origin (mountain or rain forest)
Pelomedusa subrufa **African Helmeted Turtle**	8/8 in. (20/20 cm) Few offspring in captivity	Aqua-terrarium, swimming area 3 ft. (1 m) (5 sq. ft./0.5 sq m), 12 in. (30 cm) deep, sand bottom
Terrapene carolina major **Gulf Coast Box Turtle**	8/8 in. (20/20 cm) Few offspring in captivity	Aqua-terrarium, 16 sq. ft. (1.6 sq m), 25% water portion, outdoor enclosure with pond
Testudo hermanii hermanni **Hermann's Tortoise**	6/8 in. (16/20 cm) (Smallest subspecies), offspring common in captivity	Terrarium, 15 sq. ft. (1.5 sq m)
Trachemys scripta elegans **Red-eared Slider**	8/11 in. (20/28 cm), Farm-bred offspring, mixed breeds in stores	Aquarium with at least 100 gal. (360 L) capacity, at least 5 ft. (1.5 m) long, 16 in. (40 cm) deep

Food for Adult Animals	Night/Day Temperature; also 113°F (45°C) Spotlight	Rest Periods, Special notes
Whole fish, freshly killed; dangle with tweezers	Water 73°/75°–77°F (23°/24°–25°C), UV light into the water	None/keep singly and avoid all disturbance; refuses to eat when under stress
Protein, hunts on land, about 10% plant	Air 72°/86°F (22°/30°C), preference depending on origin	Hibernation at 50°–59°F (10°–15°C) is requirement for successful breeding
Plant, high fiber, hay, occasionally insects	Air 66°/86°F (19°/30°C), no draft, over 60% humidity	Possible summer rest/active only in morning and evening
Plant, prickly pear cactus "leaves," always fresh hay	Air 72°/86°F (22°/30°C) in summer warm, winter hot, dry	None/outdoor enclosure at least 1000 sq. ft. (100 sq m) with hothouse, hiding places
Protein and plants in equal parts, active hunter	Water and air 59°/72°F (15°/22°C), test for preferred temperature	None/very territorial, usually kept singly, calm
Primarily plants, hardly any protein	Air 63°–72°F (17°–22°C)/ 77°–86°F (25°–30°C), check origin	None/active in twilight, male very territorial
Protein, active hunter in water	Air 75°–82°F (24°/28°C), check UV even in water	Summer rest buried in dirt; hibernation depending on origin
Protein, active hunter, about 30% plant	Air 72°/100°F (22°/38°C), each 2° lower in winter	Hibernation usually 3–6 weeks at 59°–64°F (15°–18°C)
Plant, field hay all year	Air 64°/81°F (18°/27°C), imitate climate of southern France	Hibernation/difficult to raise young
Primarily plant, about 20–30% protein	Water 77°/82°F (25°/28°C), bright spotlight	Hibernation at 39°–54°F (4°–12°C) for 2–3 months depending on origin

The Way Turtles
Want to Live

Today's standard for turtle care is based on the
knowledge that both enthusiasts and
scientists have discovered by keeping these animals.

The Right Accommodations for Your Turtle

A turtle poses particularly high demands on its accommodations. It wants more than a cozy terrarium in the house. It also needs an opportunity to enjoy natural sunlight on the balcony or in an outdoor enclosure.

IN ORDER FOR TURTLES to feel good and to be kept in an appropriate manner, they need a roomy terrarium or aquarium. Since various types are available in pet shops, for the sake of simplicity, they will be treated together under the term *setup* in the following pages as long as no further specifications are required.

Turtles Inside the House

Before you get a turtle, you should devote some basic thought to the appropriate accommodations.
Location: The best place is one that receives natural daylight. It should be bright, but not in the direct sun, and away from drafty doors and windows. This type of location favors the turtle's yearly cycle and plant growth—a place under a shaded glass roof, for example, in a winter garden. The change in the length of days during the course of a year has a major effect on a turtle's behavior. The length of the day is largely responsible for triggering the drive to reproduce and the start of hibernation. If natural daylight is not available, lighting must be controlled artificially. Avoid draft at all costs as

well as direct sunlight that lasts for hours. Vibrations from electrical devices (refrigerator, stereo speakers) are just as disturbing as are strong smells (tobacco smoke, air neutralizers) and noises (radio or TV).

The heaviest setup in this handbook weighs around 1320 pounds (600 kg) with 110 gallons (400 L) of water, stand, and accessories. The smallest weighs around 550 pounds (250 kg). So before you get a turtle, you should determine the expected total weight and consider that this weight is carried by four small feet. Find out in advance from your landlord or architect if the

The turtle must ▶ be able to climb over the edges of the water basin without difficulty.

▶ **1** **Young tortoises** prefer to have food and water close to their hiding place. That way they can retreat back into their hideout as soon as they are done eating and drinking.

▶ **2** **Aquatic turtles** that sun themselves on land want to be able to climb up onto land easily and get into the water quickly if danger approaches.

▶ **3** **A firmly anchored tree trunk** is needed both as a basking spot and as a place from which the aquatic turtle can easily jump into the water. It provides security and heightens the turtle's feeling of well-being.

carrying capacity of the chosen location will sustain the weight. If you rent, play it safe and ask if you can put up an aquarium or terrarium.

Size: Based on the possible ultimate size of the turtle, all specifications are given so that the setup can generally shelter a second female or a mating pair during the mating season.

Minimum size: Please always note your turtle's slightest needs. The specifications recommended here generally correspond to the ones given in professional literature. Of course, you can also first calculate the minimum size of the setup based on the present size of your turtle and expand the setup later. Once the turtle is in the larger size, you can keep the smaller terrarium as a quarantine station or a breeding basin for young animals.

Calculate the minimum requirement of a tortoise or a terrestrial swamp turtle as follows: the length and width of the terrarium equate to 5 times the turtle's eventual body length (for example, 5 × 8 inches (20 cm) = about 40 inches/1 meter) + 10 percent for the decorations. This produces an overall length and width of a little over 3 feet (1.1 m). If you multiply one dimension by the other, you get the required surface area of about 12 square feet (1.2 sq m).

With this specification in the back of your mind, you can vary the length and width of the terrarium as long as you do not go below the minimum surface area.

Two turtles: If you want to take care of a second turtle, increase the terrarium's surface area by 30 percent. This applies only to two females, though; two males always need to be kept separated.

In any case, the turtles need to be able to get away from one another. Corners and hiding places should not function as traps into which one turtle flees when the other chases it. So every hiding place needs an emergency exit. The creatures should also have the opportunity to climb around or over obstacles.

Outdoor enclosure: Do you have a large outdoor setup for your turtle? If so the setup indoors will not be used year-round, and you can use the minimum requirements.

Terrariums for Tortoises

Your tortoise's new home is con- structed like an all-glass aquarium. Whether or not your turtle feels comfortable depends not only on the proper size but mainly on how the inside is set up.

Setup

How you decorate the terrarium is crucial. Pet shops offer a good selection of possibilities. Keep in mind the notices concerning the natural habitat of the individual species (see "Profiles" on pp. 22–31).

Challenges for your pet include digging, climbing, and searching curiously with the eyes and nose. So you could set up an interesting open area in the shape of a figure eight, in which the two loops of the eight are filled with a hill and some plants.
Ground: The ground must be able to store up warmth and moisture and be rough in places so that the tortoise can wear down its claws. Good choices for

TIP

The perfect ground

The appropriate setup for a steppe terrarium, for example, for a Russian Tortoise, calls for a floor of loess or loam (from a building supplies store). When it has hardened and becomes smooth, it can be kept perfectly clean. Do not forget to put in a deep, moist corner (mixture of deciduous leaf litter and sand) for females.

the ground include deciduous leaf litter, perhaps with added bark mulch. This mixture holds moisture well. It also will not harm the tortoise if the animal occasionally eats a little of it.

Water basin: This is necessary for all species and must be adapted to the size of the tortoise. The water comes up to where the throat begins (right under

and stones to create a secure hideout for rest periods.

Extra comfort: In addition to the items already mentioned, tortoises also need a temperature gradient on the open surface of the terrarium. It should range from room temperature (64° to 68°F/18° to 20°C) to around 97°F (36°C) in the basking spot. A digging

A turtle's terrarium must be set up with the appropriate land, water, rock, and hiding place features if it is to be a good home for your pet.

the ventral shell). A low edge is important so that young tortoises in particular can climb out easily.

If the area where the terrarium is kept is unheated and if the ambient temperature is below 64°F (18°C), the water basin and the surroundings must be kept in the minimum temperature range of 64° to 68°F (18° to 20°C) with a buried heating mat and thermostat. Do not adjust this any higher. Tortoises can also get the required warmth under the spotlight.

Flat sandstone: In order to facilitate the tortoise's access to the water basin, and especially its ability to get back out, you should pave the shore with a flat piece of sandstone. Because of its abrasive nature, sandstone also helps the tortoise keep its claws worn down. In addition, the stone also keeps dirt from getting into the water. If the stone is larger than the grown tortoise, it can also be used as a feeding place.

Hiding places: Since tortoises like to hide every now and then, they need appropriate cover. So put in some roots

spot with soft, damp ground is also important.

An Aqua-terrarium for a Terrestrial Aquatic Turtle

Some species of swamp turtle spend lots of time on land. Since they also look for food on land, they need not only a roomy water area but also a large land area. Ideally, their setup will be built entirely as a glass aquarium.

A few species, such as the *Terrapene carolina*, need a large land portion right from the outset. Yet other species live primarily in the water when they are young and lay claim to the large land area only as they grow older. These include species such as *Cuora flavomarginata* and *Chinemys reevesii*. You should use the profiles in this book to get an idea of the individual demands your pet poses.

Setting up the land portion: Set the land portion right on the glass bottom. Depending on the species, the land must be 6 to 9 inches (15 to 23 cm)

◀ 1 **Commercially available** sisal ropes about 1½ inches (3 to 5 cm) thick can be used as good underwater climbing aids even in fairly tight quarters. Thinner ropes may be subject to tangling.

Robust water plants are generally spared by young aquatic turtles. That way the natural decoration remains in the aquarium and your turtle can find additional cover beneath it. 2 ▶

◀ 3 **Bogwood roots** are important decorative elements. However, your pet should not be able to get stuck under them. Fairly large pieces are well suited to herbivores that need sturdier hiding places.

The exit onto land should 4 ▶ always be simple and secure. For many species, the area on the shore will also be appreciated as a place for sunbathing.

MY PET

What temperature range does your turtle prefer?

You can find this out with the help of the temperature gradient. Your turtle's preferred temperature changes with its activity. This test will help you discover the turtle's preferences quite accurately.

The test begins:

From the time it wakes up to the time it goes to sleep, your turtle is presented with a temperature gradient with the help of a spotlight in the terrarium. Throughout the day, measure the temperatures in the places your turtle prefers to be. Write down all the times when it spends more than 3 to 5 minutes in those spots. Repeat this 3 times every 3 or 4 days to rule out chance. Adjust the terrarium temperature if necessary.

My test results:

thick and stick up over the water by about 1½ inches (3 cm).

The land is sealed off from the water. For this purpose, glue in a Plexiglas plate using aquarium silicone. It should be around 2 inches (3 to 4 cm) higher than the water level.

An Aqua-terrarium for Aquatic Turtles

For these turtles, the aqua-terrarium is nothing more than an aquarium with a lowered water portion. Here *Clemmys guttata, Emys orbicularis,* and other amphibious turtles (see "Profiles," pp. 22–31) feel at home.

The water level is adjusted to the inhabitant's requirements. If your turtle generally spends more time running around underwater than swimming (as with the genera *Knosternon, Siebenrockiella,* and *Sternotherus*), it must always be able to reach the surface of the water to breathe without having to swim. Some branches and a few loops of sisal rope about 2 inches (3 to 5 cm) thick will facilitate this movement. Cover the bottom with about a ½ inch (1 to 2 cm) of river sand.

The bottom line here is that your aqua-terrarium should be built to the precise needs of the species it will house. If you don't know the needs of your turtle, you run the risk of creating a living space that doesn't accommodate its particular requirements. This is a recipe that won't serve either you or your pet well.

Setup

For small climbers (the genera *Kinosternon*, *Siebenrockiella*, and *Sternotherus*) a cork tube should be placed at an angle in front of the land portion as an aid in getting out of the water. This is glued in horizontally between the front and back panes and kept from sliding on the land portion by means of wire. It sticks up out of the water by a third of its diameter so that an air space is inside. The tube is cut lengthwise and is open underwater so that the turtle can get into it from under the water. There it can rest and get air comfortably. Three to 5 openings around ⅜ inch (1 cm) in diameter let in the necessary fresh air.

Water Level

The water levels are specified for turtles of various species in the profiles. These are guidelines and are based on the width of the individual turtles' shell. So there must be areas in the setup in which the water is deeper than the width of the turtle. That way, if the turtle ends up on its back, it can paddle with its legs and turn itself right-side up and keep from drowning.

For babies of poor swimmers (see "Profiles," pp. 22–31), a flat shore area is ideal. You can make this by placing the aquarium onto a board and putting a piece of wood under the intake side for the filter so that there are 2 to 3 inches (5 to 7 cm) of water in the deepest spot.

Plants

Pure herbivores do not bother robust aquarium plants such as egeria, hornwort, and thread algae as long as they are not bored. Save space on the land portion by using hanging plants such as *Ficus pumila*, philodendron, and ferns that hang down from the edge of the tank and provide cover. Aquatic turtles that come onto land like roots and tufts of grass for cover.

The temperature ▶ gradient: various temperature zones and moisture gradients enrich the terrarium and are vitally important for tortoises.

20°C   38°C

An Aquarium for Aquatic Turtles

Good swimmers are happy in an aquarium with deep water and a large area for swimming. This setup is prepared much like an aqua-terrarium. The water area should be long and deep to facilitate swimming. However, make sure that the turtle cannot reach the edge of the tank or it will climb out.

Secure hiding places: Good swimmers need not only lots of open room for swimming but also a hiding place that will cover them from above. Turtles often use a suspended land portion for this purpose. Another good possibility is floating pieces of dried reed and dried leaves from cattails (flotsam). They come together to form islands that offer the creatures some cover.

A place for basking: The part of a root that sticks up out of the water below a spotlight will be used for basking as needed. The turtle must always be able to jump into deep water from this place without danger of injuring itself.

The Land Portions for an Aqua-terrarium and an Aquarium

All turtles need a land portion. With aqua-terrariums and aquariums, the land portion is suspended over the surface of the water so that the body of water is as large as possible. It is no problem if the land portion sticks into the water portion 1 to 2 inches (3 to 5 cm) as long as the turtle cannot get stuck underneath it.

The access ramp to the land must be flat and stable. The land portion should be made from $\frac{1}{8}$-inch thick (3 mm) glued-in Plexiglas plates or plastic containers. Suspend them about $\frac{1}{8}$-inch (2 to 3 mm) away from the glass on two stainless steel hangers (from a hardware store). The two hangers must reach over the edges of both ends of the aquarium glass and have a foam cushion between the hangers and the glass.

The land portion is used for basking and for laying eggs as needed. The side walls have to be high enough so that your turtle can leave the land only in the direction of the water. Otherwise, it will climb out of the aquarium wherever it can. The land portion is filled with a mixture of sand and deciduous leaf litter in equal proportions, which is always kept misty moist. The ramp or the land portion should be warmed to 104°F (40°C) with a spotlight, unless otherwise specified in the turtle profiles.

TIP

The right size for the land portion

Select a generous length by doubling or tripling the length of the grown turtle's shell. The turtle must be able to turn around easily on the land and have an opportunity to get out of the spot hot from the spotlight. The width of the ground corresponds roughly to the length of the turtle's shell.

The Appropriate Technical Accessories

The right size and setup are just a part of an installation's quality. The technical accessories adapted to the particular turtle species are at least as important.

A HIGH-QUALITY technical setup is not overly inexpensive. Do not let the cost scare you away. What you try to save at first you will pay double later on if your original purchase does not work out right. You can check the Web for information on various types of accessories.

Temperatures

Temperatures control how your turtle feels and how active it is. So pay strict attention to the recommendations in this book.

Water temperature: This is controlled by a filter with a built-in heater. In addition, or alternatively, you can provide heat with an adjustable glass aquarium heater surrounded by a protective cage.

Air temperature: Set up a temperature gradient during the day. With aquatic turtles, make sure that the air never gets colder than the water, which can happen if there is a draft. At night, turn off the lights and the spotlight.

Thermometer: A traditional laboratory thermometer (32° to 140°F/0 to 60°C) or a digital thermometer will allow you to monitor the temperature in the setup continually.

Light

Very good lighting in the setup is especially important if you have to keep your turtle indoors all year and cannot switch to an outdoor pen.

▶ Fluorescent daylight tubes: These are necessary if there is a lack of natural daylight (e.g., if the turtle is kept in the cellar). This provides the basic lighting—which the plants need, too—and is controlled by a timer switch. The duration of the lighting changes in proportion to the current length of the day.

▶ Spotlight: This additional source of light and warmth is always required. It needs to be on during the times

Flat stones glued ▶ into place with aquarium silicone provide a secure, natural ramp that your turtle will gladly use.

when your turtle is active and easily controlled with a timer switch. With 100 watts and a projection angle of 10 degrees at a distance of 3 feet (1 m), the spotlight will produce a spot about 7 inches (17 cm) in diameter with an intensity of 10,000 lux. If you hang the spotlight a little lower, 60 watts can also suffice. However, the

The UVB rays from the sun penetrate **the water**. Fifty percent will still reach floating turtles in 8 inches (20 cm) of water.

warmth-giving circle of light will be smaller. The spotlight is primarily a source of warmth. Usually it also serves as a light source for mud turtles (*Sternotherus, Kinosternon*).

▸ UV light: This is required for turtles that are kept indoors exclusively. Every day it must be turned on with a timer switch for the first activity period of the day. It should be on for about 20 minutes and from a distance of about 32 inches (80 cm). It is also needed for about 10 minutes for the second activity period. UV light (= sunlight) is very important for bone growth and the formation of a healthy carapace. Even turtles that are active in the twilight bask in the morning or evening sun. From experience, I can recommend only one lamp type: Ultra-Vitalux, 300 watt, from Osram (face-tanner) or an identical lamp from some other manufacturer (Philipps, Sylvania).

Other types of lamps such as HQL or mixed-light lamps, have a negligible UV yield and distribution. Check the Internet if you need further information about types of lighting.

▸ Halogen-metal vapor lamps: These mainly meet the lighting needs of painted turtles, *Emydura, Emys,* and tortoises that are kept indoors year-round. There are quartz and ceramic bulbs as well as mercury vapor pressure lamps. Quarts bulbs (150 watts) produce 13,000 lumens, which comes very close to daylight. Mercury vapor pressure lamps (125 watts) produce 6200 lumens.

Make sure to adjust the lighting intensity to the season by hanging the lamp around 32 inches (80 cm) above the setup in the summer but significantly higher (up to 54 inches/1.5 m) in the spring and fall.

Filter

Choose a filter that is as large as possible and has a canister volume of 12 to 18 quarts/liters. That way, even with small amounts to be filtered, you end up with a usable total volume.

A pump for an aquarium moves around 600 quarts/liters per hour. It is turned down according to the manufacturer's instructions so that it cycles the contents of the aquarium once every hour. The outflow inside the aquarium is provided with a standard protective mesh. A drain should be in the glass bottom. Install a common drain with a ball valve in the hole. This lets you optimize the flow from the filter. Later on, you will be very grateful for this practical way to empty the tank.

Technical Accessories
at a Glance

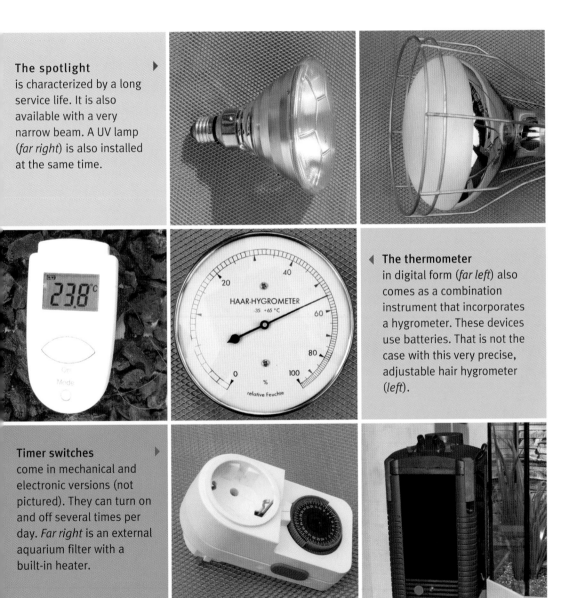

The spotlight ▶
is characterized by a long service life. It is also available with a very narrow beam. A UV lamp (*far right*) is also installed at the same time.

◀ **The thermometer**
in digital form (*far left*) also comes as a combination instrument that incorporates a hygrometer. These devices use batteries. That is not the case with this very precise, adjustable hair hygrometer (*left*).

Timer switches ▶
come in mechanical and electronic versions (not pictured). They can turn on and off several times per day. *Far right* is an external aquarium filter with a built-in heater.

Outdoor Accommodations

Outdoor installations cannot be replaced by technical devices. Natural sunlight, a variety of stimuli from the environment, and opportunities to swim and climb increase the turtle's vitality and cannot be duplicated indoors.

IN TEMPERATE LATITUDES, outdoor living generally is possible only in the months of June through August. With a hothouse—as appropriate to the species—it may go on for 1 to 3 months longer. Check the recommendation on outdoor living in the profile section.

An Outdoor Setup in the Yard

Use the illustrations on page 45 to inspire you to come up with your own design that is appropriate to your yard. Track the location of the sun through the year so that the setup is exposed to sunlight as long as possible, especially in the morning. Mark off the outline with surveyor's tape and note—perhaps over the course of 6 months—if and when it comes under shadows from buildings and trees. You can also start with a temporary board fence that can be easily moved to sunny spots and adjusted. You will then quickly find out if your turtle will make good use of the offering. If so, make the setup permanent. For cold days, you will also need a spotlight. The positive effects of this measure will demonstrate themselves in the livelier, more active behavior of your turtle. In the early spring or fall, the turtle must be cared for indoors when it is not hibernating, unless a small greenhouse is part of the outdoor installation.

An Outdoor Installation with Berry Bushes

Let grass and weeds (e.g., dandelion, chickweed) grow in the enclosure. Plant berry bushes (raspberries and black and red currants, small juniper bushes, blackberries, and hawthorn). Right up through the fall, they will occasionally drop ripe berries. Every turtle is happy to look for and find something. In addition, the bushes provide shade for tortoises on hot summer days. If many berries are lying about on the ground, remove the surplus every day. The berries could ferment and make your turtle drunk, or they could get moldy.

Compost Piles as Food Dispensers

Set up a small compost pile in a partly shady area inside the outdoor installation for swamp turtles that spend a lot of time on land (*Cuora*, *Chinemys*). Surround it with rotten, untreated wood under which small creatures of all kinds—isopods, earthworms, grubs, bugs, and millipedes—will quickly come to live. Your turtle will soon hunt there. If it prefers not to come out of the water, simply toss the small creatures into the pond as a treat. The turtle will be grateful for the meal.

A Setup for Tortoises

The bigger you design the outdoor pen, the more harmoniously it will fit into your yard. That is because of the possibility of concealing the fence and the hothouse with bushes and using your imagination with the landscaping. An area of 29 square yards (25 sq m) should be sufficient for two tortoises. The absolute minimum width for the pen should be 4 feet (1.2 m), with a length of 10 feet (3 m). If it is smaller, the grass and weeds suffer, and the ground becomes bare. The ground inside the pen needs to be about 1 foot (30 cm) lower than the level of the yard. The ground must have a slope of about 2 inches per yard (5 cm per m). A hill integrated into the enclosure will be used for basking and laying eggs. In addition, it will protect the tortoise from high water resulting from a downpour. At the lowest spot must be a drain into the yard for rainwater.

The surrounding wall is made of palisades, waterproof plywood, or corrugated fiber cement (from a building supplies store). In the store you can also find out how to set in the palisade enclosure or place the plywood on a foundation strip. Generally, a height of 16 inches (40 cm) should be adequate. In no case should the tortoise be able to reach the top edge with its

2 **A comfortable greenhouse** with a turtle pond provides an ideal habitat for aquatic turtles. The broad, shallow shore warms up easily and stays warm for a long time with the help of solar heating.

▼

▲

1 **An outdoor enclosure** for tortoises is complete only with a hothouse and additional heating (spotlight). This complementary equipment also provides the tortoise with protection in case of an unexpected cold snap.

To get through cold days, **install a spotlight** (60 to 80 watts) in the cold frame; it should reach a temperature of around 104°F (40°C) on the ground.

front feet, even when it climbs onto a root or another tortoise. The 20-inch (50 cm) foundation or palisades sunk to the same depth are protection against escape tunnels. If your tortoises are shorter than 4 inches (10 cm) and correspondingly lightweight, the outdoor enclosure needs to be covered with bird netting. Otherwise the tortoises will be easy prey for crows and magpies. As protection against rats, lock your tortoises into the greenhouse at night.

A Backyard Pond/Outdoor Setup for Aquatic Turtles

This requires slightly different rules than does the traditional backyard pond. The differences involve the location—ideally sunny all day long—and the form. I recommend my special sombrero design, with a broad rim and a deep part in the middle. This best

Bark caves quickly become too small if they were not originally made large enough.
▼

satisfies the turtle's needs for warm-water areas. You can also include solar heating.

The ideal pond configuration: If you have enough room, a diameter of about 20 feet (6 m) is ideal. If you do not have the room, of course it can be smaller. The level shore should be 6 feet (2 m) wide. In the middle is a 3-foot-deep (1 m) spot 6 feet (2 m) across. This produces a pond with a capacity of about 55 cubic feet (5.6 cu m), including nearly 45 cubic feet (4 cu m) near the shore, which quickly warms up in the sun. There is about a 7-degree slope from the shore to the center of the pond. Then it goes into the deep part as steeply as possible (45 to 50 degrees). Use a pond liner so that you can reproduce the shape easily, and just leave the black liner as it is. This encourages solar warming. Plant cattails or reeds in the center in a pan filled with sand. Decorate the shallow-water areas with good-sized tree trunks (from water bodies in the wild) as basking islands.

Proper filtration: If you are keeping two or three turtles in this installation, a filter is superfluous since the water can process the organic contamination from three animals during the summer. If necessary, you can water your lawn with the water from the deep area in the middle (where most of the waste collects) and add freshwater (a partial water change). If you put in a pond filter, choose a pump that can handle from about 70 to 140 gallons (250 to 500 L) an hour. Pump up the water from the deepest part, and let it run back into the center where the reeds are.

As a return from the filter, use 60 to 90 feet (20 to 30 m) of black plastic hose laid out in a place that is sunny all day long, preferably on a black piece of corrugated metal. That way, the water gets warmed before flowing back into the pond, even on cloudy days (the solar heating principle).

around it. This will also keep house pets (dogs or cats) and children from falling in and possibly drowning.

Cold frame: Set up a cold frame with Plexiglas panes (available ready to install in gardening supply shops). This will store up sufficient warmth through the greenhouse effect even during periods of bad weather.

DID YOU KNOW THAT . . .

. . . a great number of exotic pet turtles die every year?

This happens because they are forced to hibernate in backyard ponds. The first warm spell wakes them up at the beginning of March, but cold snaps as late as May keep the turtles from digesting their food properly. It goes bad in their digestive tract. Along with a lung infection and the impossibility of reaching their preferred temperature, this amounts to their death sentence.

Preventing escapes: The tortoise pond in the outdoor installation is secured with a perimeter fence. Make the surface of the pond around 16 inches (40 cm) lower than the yard. You can also pile up dirt from the outside against the enclosure so that the wall is less obvious.

If necessary, you can secure the pond by putting a common garden fence

Access for the tortoise is provided by an opening with a hinged flap. You can use a cat door. Install this access so that the tortoise can get in by itself when it moves against the edge.

Aquatic turtles do not need a flap. They get into the shelter from underneath, about a quarter of the lower edge sticks out into the pond water. It goes in an inch or two (a few centimeters) so that no draft can get in.

◀ Small outlay, big effect: A setup on a balcony allows your turtle to bask in the sunshine.

An Outdoor Setup on a Terrace or Balcony

If you do not have an appropriate yard, how about a sunny terrace or a balcony? These are other places where you can set up an outdoor enclosure for your turtle. It will contain the same features matched to the biology of the individual species—the dimensions and the accessories—as an indoor installation. However, it does not have supplementary lighting (see illustration above).

A Setup for Tortoises

Imagine the whole installation as a planted cold frame modified to serve as a terrarium. Set it up on your terrace or balcony in such a way that even when the sun is low, the light will shine through the slanted glass roof onto the floor of the enclosure. The body of the cold frame is made of wood, preferably of pressure-treated fence laths (from a building supplies store).

Filling: First put in about $\frac{1}{8}$ inch (20 cm) layer of expanded clay (from a gardening supplies store) followed by a layer of potting soil. Put a standard root barrier between the expanded clay and the dirt to serve as an underlay for the pond liner. That will keep a digging tortoise from forcing its way down to the expanded clay. The clay functions as a moisture retainer that feeds the dirt through upward capillary action.

Put in only enough dirt so that the tortoise cannot climb out. To keep the wood from rotting, line the box with pond liner before filling it up. Poke a couple of holes in the part of the liner that covers the floor to allow excess water to drain out.

Cover: The whole setup is covered with two panes of Plexiglas held in a frame. This should be open up to the eaves so that rainwater can run off easily. Also cut the sides of the box on an angle so that the front is 4 to 6 inches (10 to 15 cm) lower than the rear. When the

Plexiglas sheets are in place, it is like a desktop that the sun easily shines through. The panes are removed in the sunshine and put back into place in cold weather. In your absence, an adjustable temperature control device can also accomplish this, as commonly used to regulate simple ventilation flaps in small greenhouses. A couple of ¾-inch (2 cm) air holes drilled into the wood assure that there is ventilation even if the panes are closed for several days. When the panes are closed, keep an eye on the thermometer. Covering over the part of the glass top under which your tortoise has set up a resting place prevents additional heat buildup and provides security. As a safety measure, seal up any spaces along the floor of the balcony with boards to keep any tortoise that gets out of the box from suffering a fall.

Preventing draft: One rarely considered danger is draft on high balconies. It generally occurs even when there is no wind on the ground. In such cases, secure your enclosure with a wind screen.

Plants for a balcony setup: Plants that reach a height greater than 8 to 12 inches (20 to 30 cm) will not fit into a turtle installation on a balcony. So plant tall berry and fruit bushes in pots. Place these pots close to the enclosure so that the branches reach over part of the setup and the berries or fruits can fall inside. This will make the tortoise happy.

An Enclosure for Aquatic Turtles

The enclosure is basically the same as the one for tortoises. To create a pond for your aquatic turtle, put in a mortar tray and add all the details such as water depth and underwater accessories in accordance with the specifications for an indoor aquarium. Filter and empty the water through a drain in the bottom, as described for an aquarium. This has the advantage of allowing you to use the filter on the balcony. The filter material is the same. It is broken in and can continue to function. Plant and decorate the enclosure as described in the aquarium section.

A Greenhouse

During the last 30 years, our understanding of the demands posed by a turtle kept in captivity has increased dramatically. The result: keeping a turtle responsibly involves providing it with the same quality of life as in its home environment. This is best accomplished with a small greenhouse. For example, in Greece, the turtles are active and mating as early as February. Sometimes they are also outdoors as late as the beginning of December. This means that they make do with 2 to 3 months of hibernation. In more

---

TIP

Effective filter material

In my experience, a combination of about 1½ inches (4 cm) each of fine fleece (strainer) and large-pored filter matting of the same material (from a specialty shop) has served well as a carrier of the microorganisms that break down dissolved food substances. Rinse the strainer material every 14 days in cold water and the coarse filter every 2 to 3 months.

◀ *This illustration shows a typical turtle greenhouse.*

the cold season because of sunlight flooding in (the greenhouse effect). A small exit with a hinged flap lets the turtle take short excursions outdoors on nice days as early as March or April.

Climate control: Whether you set up a freestanding greenhouse or a half-greenhouse that leans against the wall, it needs ventilation and shade. With a leaning greenhouse, the wall of the house stores up heat and makes it easier to get heat, electricity, and water into it from the house. Ideally, the greenhouse should be on the east side of the house to avoid an excess of sunshine. The greenhouse is glazed with double-ribbed polycarbonate panes that let no UVB light through. Under these conditions, your turtle will get enough UV rays outdoors.

Double-glazed panes have adequate insulating value. An automatically adjustable skylight opener (with temperature sensor and pneumatic spring) will prevent heat buildup.

When constructing the green-house, observe the techniques that engineers use for controlling light and temperature inside greenhouses. First, slats must be installed on the outside that provide effective protection against sun and resultant heat buildup. Simultaneously, they must hold back around 70 percent of the incoming light. A less costly interior shade—like an inside venetian blind or a standard shade for greenhouses—filters out 50 percent of the light but lets the heat in.

temperate zones, hibernation can last for 6 months (from November to the beginning of April) and thus last 3 to 4 months longer. This does not harm the turtle at all, but the greenhouse could be used to optimize its active time.

How it works: In many temperate areas during the summer, there can be temperature drops of 35°F (20°C), for example, from 85° to 50°F (30° to 10°C) and lots of rain. Summer in many places, in comparison with the homeland of most turtles, is excessively cool and damp. A greenhouse balances this out and provides climatic conditions like those of Greece. The turtle can also go into its hibernation nook by itself and rest there until the end of February. This is possible because the right climate is present inside the greenhouse even in

Planting with deciduous trees is economical and effective. That way, the house is shaded in the summer but heated by the sun in the spring.

The minimum recommended size is 6 feet on each side (2 × 2 × 2 m). Depending on local regulations, greenhouses that exceed a certain size or volume may require a permit from the building authorities. Check your local requirements.

What species? You can keep warmth-loving species such as the Box Turtle and Indian Star Tortoise in a greenhouse from the spring through late summer because producing the appropriate climate inside it is easy. You can even use a mister on warm days to create the right microclimate that allows the Yellow-margined Painted Turtle and the Indian Star Tortoise to take short excursions outdoors.

2 **Bark mulch and deciduous leaf litter** store up moisture, provide insulation against a cold ground, and do not produce constipation if the turtle occasionally eats a couple of pieces.

▼

1 **The Pancake Tortoise can climb up** vertical cliffs. Opportunities for climbing surely keep them fit inside the terrarium, but they must never be allowed to climb out of the pen.

Questions About
Accommodations

? **We have some old, overgrown branches on our fruit tree. Can these be used as climbing aids for a turtle in an aquarium?**

Basically, you can immerse any kind of wood in your aquarium. You can do this under only one condition: it must be leached clean. In other words, there must be no traces of sap left. First remove the bark. Then leach the branches under water in a brook or your backyard pond until they no longer show any water mold in the form of cottony coatings. Fresh branches as thick as a person's arm must be leached for around 3 to 4 months. Then they can be put into the aquarium. They do not last as long as bogwood. However, under water with no air contact, they will last 3 to 5 years, and the outer layer slowly peels off.

? **Our tortoise is free to use the yard in the summer; we have a tortoise-proof fence. The tortoise drinks from our backyard pond, but I am afraid it may fall in. Can tortoises swim and get back out of the pond?**

Generally, tortoises swim so poorly that I prefer to answer your question with "No." A broad, gradual shore around the pond is thus the best strategy for keeping the creature from drowning. Most fatal accidents occur because a swimming turtle cannot get back onto land because the edge is too high. If an accident should happen, first aid consists of holding the turtle head downward and shaking the turtle carefully to let the water run out of its lungs. This is one way to bring turtles that appear to be dead back to life.

? **Why should I not put my young turtle into the terrarium with the old one? They get along fine and even eat the same food.**

The food is the problem! Turtles do not see clearly right in front of their nose. If your little and big turtles bite the same food simultaneously, the large one might bite the little one on the head or even bite off its whole head. The harder the adult turtle bites, the more likely this is to happen. In order to avoid this type of accident, keep older and younger creatures separate.

? **Somebody recommended an infrared ceramic lamp for my turtle's sunbath; it would last a lot longer than a spotlight. Can I use it?**

A turtle is drawn to the

sunlight to get warm. It associates warmth with this light when it is looking for warmth. However, it cannot recognize the infrared light from a distance when you turn it on. Thus, an infrared light is not very helpful.

? I put a cork island for basking into the water for my baby Slider. However, the turtle never uses it. How come?

You will see that the cork island always moves away when your turtle tries to climb up onto it. This tires your animal unnecessarily. Provide a solid foundation from a piece of root that sticks up out of the water. You can instead fasten the cork bark securely with stiff wire or glue it between the front and back panes.

? Isn't 100° to 104°F. (38° to 40°C) too hot for a basking place?

The temperature corresponds to the true temperature of dry ground in the full sun in the wild. The turtle will not stay there long. It is more likely to seek partial shade for basking. Therefore, there must be sufficient room around the hot spot for the turtle to lie in the margin. If it continues to avoid the center, move the spotlight gradually higher until the turtle can use the center of the hot spot.

? Can I put my aquatic turtle in with fish?

This will work with species of turtle that swim poorly—but mostly in theory. The water must always have the quality of aquarium water. In the long run, you can achieve this only if your aquarium contains more than 100 gallons (400 L) of water and you have only one turtle. Then you must adjust the water temperature as well as possible for both the fish and the turtle. The fish need cover to get away safely from the turtle. Overall, I do not recommend this.

? My tortoise likes to run around on the floor. So why should it not do this?

In an outdoor installation, the ground is almost always warmer than you think and especially warmer than your floor. Even with radiant floor heating, there is a major difference: the ground continually draws the heat. That harms your turtle. It can easily pick up a lung infection.

Welcome
Home

Taking care of a turtle is a beautiful and exciting responsibility.
However, it can turn into an unexpected adventure if you do not
think things over carefully before getting a turtle.

It Is Time to Get a Turtle

Once you have carefully prepared the setup for your turtle, there is nothing to keep your new ward from moving in. When buying the creature and bringing it home, take the necessary care to avoid unpleasant surprises.

YOU CANNOT LOSE if before buying your turtle, you get as much information as possible about the responsibilities you are about to take on. Clubs for turtle enthusiasts are a big help with this. In addition, you can find answers to specific questions from scientifically based turtle organizations on the Internet.

What to Look for When Purchasing

Where and when to buy? You can get turtles from pet shops, which generally sell offspring from private parties, or directly from the breeders. Good dealers keep their turtles in such a way that you have the impression that they have complied with the basic rules for housing and feeding. In addition, they can answer your questions about the turtle's feeding, species, and age. They can also describe the basic required living conditions. Calmly test the dealer with detailed questions. Of course, he or she must be able to produce any required documents for protected species. Under such conditions, you should be able to count on purchasing a

healthy turtle now and getting advice from the dealer later on.

Buying from a breeder has another advantage: you get a direct look into the living conditions for a turtle operation. You can get an idea of the technical accessories and space requirements. In addition, you can benefit from the breeder's great experience.

Notice: You can occasionally get for free adult specimens of species in which the females grow to be 10 or 12 inches (25 to 30 cm) long, such as many Painted Turtles and Sliders. You can get them from animal shelters, zoos, or animal collection stations. All kinds of animals

A carrying crate with a damp fiber rug is a very good way to transport a young aquatic turtle.

Hand feeding makes it easier for you to check
your pet's health.

have been abandoned by their former
"fans."

When to buy? Experience shows that it
is best to buy a turtle in May or August.
Then hibernation is over and the
creature is already exhibiting lively
behavior. Another advantage: you have
time to get the turtle acclimated to
living with you. You can watch its
health until the next hibernation (if
applicable) and take care of any
treatments. If you buy a turtle in the
fall, there will not be enough time for
this. If you get an animal in March or
April, right after it comes out of
hibernation, you will not be able to tell
if its behavior is normal or if it has
become ill during hibernation and its
illness is now just blossoming.

Note: Under no circumstances
should you buy your turtle from a
bazaar, a flea market, or on the Internet.

Making the Right Choice

As for the species, this book has
provided a preliminary screening for
you. It is especially important that the
species purchased is bred in the latitude
in which you live. Even as a beginner,
you will be well served if you use the
mentioned criteria as a basis for your
selection.

Buying offspring bred in captivity: In
addition to considerations of species
protection, this has the great advantage
of affording you a chance to ask the
breeder about the precise living
conditions for the turtle. This is
especially helpful with species that
have an extensive north-to-south
distribution. In other words, the
northern populations live in cooler
regions than their southern relatives
and may hibernate. Since this is
genetically programmed, this type of
creature in your care should also be able
to pull back during the winter. This
applies, for example, to the Spotted
Turtle and the Yellow-margined Painted
Turtle.

With successful breeding, the
breeder has already demonstrated a
precise knowledge of the preferred
temperature range and the true
hibernation needs of your turtle.

Animals from a breeder have
another advantage: they are free of
injuries that could result from long-
distance transport. As a layperson,
you may first become aware of shipping
damage when the turtle stops eating,
becomes apathetic, and needs urgent
treatment by a veterinarian for some
problems.

Old or Young Turtle?

Turtles from a breeder are usually young animals. Raising them is a challenge. It is easier to acclimate an adolescent or adult turtle whose bone structure has already formed. There is also nothing wrong with purchasing a healthy, adult turtle that has already been kept as a pet for many years.

Male, Female, or Both?

The males of some aquatic turtle species remain smaller than the females. This could be important to you if you do not have room for a large terrarium. If you want to keep several animals, you must consider that you cannot put two males of any species together or put a mating pair together for a long time. However, it is possible to put two females of the same species together— as long as they are from one of the peaceable species.

My tip: As a beginner, you should start with one turtle. A turtle needs no company from others of its kind in order to be happy. With increasing experience, you may wish to breed turtles. I then advise you to form a breeding cooperative with other turtle owners. This saves each partner from additional expense.

Starting with an Ad

As you search for a turtle, you will encounter unknown abbreviations and technical terms in ads and price lists. Here are the most important ones:

Technical Terms in Ads

- ▸ 1.0 means a male.
- ▸ 0.2 means two females.
- ▸ 1.1 means a mating pair.

- ▸ Juv. means young animal (from Latin *juvenalis*).
- ▸ Adult means sexually mature.
- ▸ Subadult means shortly before reaching sexual maturity.

Male or Female

▸ 1 **The sexes** can be distinguished by the length of the tail. At the left in the top photo is a male with a long tail; at right, a female with a short tail.

▸ 2 **On their front feet,** sexually mature Sliders (*left* in the photo above) have especially long claws, which are used in courtship. With females (*right*), the claws are much less pronounced.

A HEALTH CHECK FOR
YOUR TURTLE

	Healthy	Sick
Weight	A healthy turtle feels like a stone of the same size in your hand.	The turtle is noticeably lighter than a stone of the same size.
Activity	Young turtles flail with their front and back legs when they are picked up; adults pull back into their shell (different defensive behavior).	When they are picked up, the animals act apathetic and let their head and legs hang down.
Eyes	They are clear and wide open.	The cornea is cloudy, and the lids are swollen.
Eardrum	This is located behind the eye and is smooth.	The eardrum bulges outward.
Nose	There is no discharge or bubbles, and the breathing is silent.	There are bubbles on the nose, and the breathing is noisy.
Inside of Mouth	The inside of the mouth is pink and free of pale or other coatings.	The inside of the mouth is dark red, with a visible coating on the mucous membranes.
Limbs	Front and hind legs are firm.	Front and hind legs are noticeably swollen or gaunt.
Vent	Around the vent, the skin is clean, smooth, and free of injury.	The region around the vent is swollen or injured.
Shell	The shell shows no damage, and there are no scars. With young turtles, the shell is firm but resilient under pressure.	The joints in the shell are pink and inflamed; injuries or holes exude secretions and smell bad. The shell feels soft under pressure.

Moving into the New House

Safe transportation home and patient acclimation will give your turtle a good start in its new home. The quarantine takes some time but is very important for the turtle.

HERE IS WHERE THINGS STAND: You have decided on a specific turtle and are now a proud owner.

The Trip Home

You can get an appropriate transport container from a pet shop or a breeder during the warm months.

▸ For tortoises and aquatic turtles that are already adolescents, this will be a cloth bag. This bundle is put into a tightly fitting box to keep the turtle from sliding around. Several layers of crumpled newspaper will absorb shocks.

▸ Young aquatic turtles are transported in small plastic boxes. A carpet of damp terry cloth is put in. Tear a second piece of terry cloth into 2-inch squares (5 × 5 cm), and put these over the animal.

You now have a transportation container with water storage, and your pet will feel secure under the pieces of terry cloth. Now comes a cover, and everything is ready for a trip of 3 to 6 hours.

If the weather is fairly cold or hot, you can get a Styrofoam box with a lid to hold the transportation container. In the winter, put in a hot-water bottle at

86°F (30°C) and wrap up both loosely in a light wool blanket. In my experience, it is adequate for transporting the creature for 1 to 3 hours even through frigid weather.

My tip: Keep your transportation container. If necessary, you can use it to take your turtle to the veterinarian. You can also use it again, if you clean it appropriately, to transport other turtles to your home in the future.

Is the turtle fit and trim? You must weigh the turtle regularly to check its nutrition.
▼

The quarantine terrarium for young aquatic turtles that are not good swimmers should have a gently sloping shore. You can achieve this by putting a piece of wood under one side.

Quarantine

At first glance, you cannot tell if a turtle has worms or an infection. Even the breeder or pet shop owner cannot guarantee the turtle's condition. Until that is determined, the turtle has to start out in a quarantine tank.

The Quarantine Tank

This can either be a regular aquarium or a terrarium that will later be used for raising young animals or be simply a square basin made of black plastic (a mortar tray from a hardware store). In either case, the tank should have a capacity of about 16 to 40 gallons (60 to 140 L), depending on the size of your pet.

For the setup of the tank, the same guidelines apply as for the indoor enclosure. The technical accessories are also the same. If necessary, the water can be heated with a shatterproof aquarium wand heater (from a pet shop). For the 2 to 3 weeks of quarantine, UV light is not necessary.

A tortoise gets its first lukewarm bath with a solution of ⅓ ounce of physiological salt per quart (9 g per 1 L). Then the tortoise can move into the quarantine tank. This is outfitted with a cork tube for a hiding place and tufts of grass for grazing and climbing around on.

An aquatic turtle is simply placed into the water in the quarantine tank. For good swimmers, the tank is filled halfway with water. Poor swimmers are provided with a water level slightly deeper than the breadth of their shell and a gently sloping shore. You can place a piece of wood under one side of the aquarium (see illustration above).

Care in Quarantine

The turtle stays in quarantine until a veterinarian confirms that it is free of health problems.

If the creature is shy at first and hides, let it stay in its hiding place until it willingly comes out. Remove any food that it does not eat before the food goes bad. Leaving rotten food around can make your turtle sick.

Getting a fecal sample: In the first days after the turtle's arrival, you should get a fecal sample. Your veterinarian can give you specific recommendations and special containers for the droppings. An examination of the droppings will reveal if intestinal parasites that cannot be detected with the naked eye are present.

Sometimes turtle droppings are so soft that they dissolve in water and you cannot get a sample. Place the creature onto a moist underlay in a different container, and let it leave droppings. It is important to have these checked by a veterinarian, so keep trying until you obtain a usable sample.

Building Trust

Your first commandment is to set aside some time for your turtle. Do not pester it, and respect its rest times. Make contact with it only during the times when it is active.

Getting the Turtle Used to Being Picked Up

In order to inspect your pet closely, you need to pick it up. Get it used to this touching by holding out a couple of pieces of food in your hand. Soon the turtle will cease to associate the proximity of your hand with danger and, rather, with an offer of a

MY PET

What is the aquatic turtle's favorite hiding place?

For their midday and nightly rest, turtles withdraw into a secure hiding place. The preferences are very different depending on species. Does your aquatic turtle prefer underwater cavities or a "mud" of foam packing peanuts?

The test begins:

Put a long cork tube into the enclosure for poor swimmers (except for Matamatas). Leave half of it empty, and fill the other part halfway with foam packing peanuts (about 1 inch/3 cm on an edge). If the tube is short, use two pieces. Good swimmers can also choose a flotsam island. Your turtle will first inspect all hiding places and then choose one. Make this type of enclosure available continuously.

My test results:

Teaching Children Responsibility

Our seven-year old daughter really enjoys her tortoise. We have some reservations, though, because in her enthusiasm, she wants to leave the turtle on the floor in her play farm. Do you have any advice on how I can do the right thing for my daughter and the turtle?

IT IS A CRUCIAL STEP in the life of a child to learn that a turtle is not a toy but, rather, a creature with its own living requirements that must be satisfied. I have been able to motivate children by diverting their impulse to play into responsible actions. You can do this, too.

Informative Reading Time

First tell your daughter in your own, easy-to-understand words some interesting information about the life of a turtle.

Taking a Look at Terrariums

The next step involves having your child experience how this type of story transfers to the real life of a turtle. Take the time to observe the terrarium of a tortoise or an aquatic turtle in a zoo for a couple of hours and explain behavior patterns, such as searching for food, basking, reproduction, and the attendant space requirements.

Many zoos offer special courses for children through their educational department. Ask about them. An alternative to the zoo is the members of a terrarium club and perhaps also breeders, who will certainly be glad to explain their setup.

The Setup

If your daughter continues to show interest, it is time for the big reward. Get the terrarium, and allow your child to set up the enclosure under your continually expert direction and with the help of this book. Generally, you will be amazed that your daughter has forgotten nothing important, for she has already "internalized" the turtle's needs.

If anything is missing, help her a little. For example, use pointed questions such as, Where can the turtle hide? Where can it go to get warm? After these first experiences, which heighten empathy with the life of a turtle, your daughter will have long given up the idea of keeping the turtle in a toy farm. You have succeeded, presumably, but of course you must still always be on hand with advice for any possible relapses.

nourishing treat. When you pick up a turtle, you must hold it securely, especially if it is a side-neck turtle, which will startle you by flailing around with its head or by snapping.

Getting Two Turtles Used to One Another

The time for courtship and mating in the spring (or sometimes in the fall) is the best time to put a sexually mature pair together. This applies to both tortoises and aquatic turtles. For this purpose, an extensive outdoor enclosure in which the creatures can get away from each other works well.

Putting sexually mature turtles together makes sense only if you want to form a breeding group with several females. However, you should do this outside the time for courtship and laying eggs.

The adjustment to one another must take place only under your constant supervision. If you have any doubts, use a board to partition the enclosure into two halves temporarily during your absence, with one turtle in each half. If the creatures simply do not get along, you will have to keep them in separate enclosures.

Turtles and Other Pets

There are lots of stories of dogs and cats biting or playing with turtles out of curiosity. So always remain close by when animals that are enemies of turtles in the wild meet a turtle. Hamsters, mice, guinea pigs, and songbirds pose no danger.

Turtles and Children

From the age of 6, children watch very closely and can take proper care of a turtle with adult supervision. As children grow older, they know what measures are needed to provide appropriate living conditions. They grow to be responsible turtle experts and do not turn their armored pet into a cuddle toy.

Turtles do not always get along on small basking islands. Many chase their opponent away by biting.

Good Food Keeps a Turtle Fit and Healthy

Feeding a turtle properly is facilitated by scientific principles.
Still, providing appropriate, balanced nutrition
remains a very important task.

The Right Food— Copied from Nature

What nature serves up for turtles can be described as a complete diet. The food contains all the important components without making the turtle fat. Feeding a turtle in the house in the same healthy way is the major challenge for every owner.

TO FEED YOUR TURTLE the right foods, you should know what it eats in the wild.

Tortoises: The species that live in the Mediterranean region find grasses, herbs, fruit-bearing bushes (junipers), prickly pear cacti, berries, and mushrooms in their territory.

Terrestrial aquatic turtles: They eat a mixed diet on land. That is, they eat both the herbs that grows there, as do tortoises, and small creatures. They find the latter on the land in the form of insects (crickets, grasshoppers, bugs, and their larvae), spiders, isopods, earthworms, slugs, snails, and millipedes. They also will not pass up carrion.

Aquatic turtles: In the wild, they find lots of small creatures in the water: crustaceans (water fleas), insects and their larvae (water bugs, mosquito larvae), mollusks (snails and mussels), carrion from fish, mammals, birds, whole young fish, and amphibians and their larvae (tadpoles). With age, many aquatic turtle species change in varying degrees from pure protein eaters to omnivores (see "Profiles," pp. 22–31). Others, such as the Painted Turtle, eat water plants exclusively.

Basic Food from Nature

Nature also supplies you with an easily accessible basic food for your tortoise: pasture hay. It has a positive effect on the digestive process. The droppings remain firm, and the fiber content cleans out the intestine.

Hay—a stockpile of food: When grass is cut in full bloom, it dries to hay with about 12 percent protein and 20 to 30 percent fiber content. In pet shops, you can get hay from mountain meadows in fairly small packages. You can also get hay directly from farmers. It must be dry, because damp hay will make your turtle sick. Hay can be supplemented

TIP

Leaves as treats

Since the 1980s, I have been giving tortoises in the zoo cuttings from common maple, whitehorn, young birch and hornbeam and leaves from grapevines to supplement their diet. The latter are appropriate only if they have never been sprayed. Leaves are best if they come from your own garden.

with vegetables and greens such as Chinese cabbage, purslane, or other leaves and vegetables in season (e.g., broccoli). This produces a good emergency mix just in case you cannot put together fresh food every day.

You can also buy thick, pressed pellets made from dried, ground hay. Before feeding, the pellets must be

The best supplemental food for tortoises is **fresh, dry hay** that smells like tea.

softened for a half hour in enough water to produce a thick gruel. Otherwise, water removal in the turtle's intestine can lead to dangerous blockages.

In my experience, sensory experience for turtles is limited. At least my animals in the zoo needed a lot of coaxing to accept this food.

The Right Way to Feed Tortoises

At the end of the 1990s, scientific studies revealed that the ideal feeding has to take into account the nutritional content in the dry substance. An adult tortoise thus needs:

▸ 20% plant protein (24% for young animals),
▸ less than 10% of crude plant fat,
▸ 12 to 30% crude fiber,
▸ 2% lime (calcium), and
▸ 1.2% phosphorus.

Overall, the selection and composition of the food should provide a ratio of calcium to phosphorus of 1.5:1 or 2:1. The food should thus contain significantly more calcium than phosphorus. On the basis of these specifications, you can identify a proper food by reading the nutritional label. You can also check the data for the standard food mixes for tortoises. If you do not find these data on the packaging, play it safe and do not purchase that food.

Note: The nutritional values should not vary significantly from the ones listed above.

The Safe Standard Mix

As a point of reference, here is an example of a simple food mixture with the above-mentioned portions of proteins to phosphorus—of course in the proper proportions:

▸ 80% romaine lettuce,
▸ 12% apple,
▸ 5% banana, and
▸ 1% each of other fruits, carrots, and dandelion.

You can vary the menu by substituting local wild herbs such as goatsfoot, chickweed, and various species of plantain. Other welcome plant foods include white and red clover, Anne Greenway spotted dead nettle, stinging nettle, bindweed, and spring vetch. They can be given alone or in the mixture.

The Right Diet for Omnivores

First check the profiles (see pp. 22–31) for the proportions of plant material and animal protein your turtle eats—whether equal proportions (50:50), primarily plant food (75:25), or mainly protein (25:75). Note that this

Good Food
at a Glance

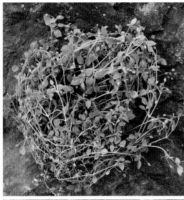

Wild Plants

Fresh, first cut hay, (*far left*), and chickweed (*left*) are good foods for tortoises. They contain a healthy surplus of calcium in correct ratio with the phosphorus.

Foliage

Fresh leaves from blackberries (*right*) are available nearly year-round, including winter. Young birch leaves (*far right*) are also favorites among tortoises.

Special Treats

Leaves of stinging nettles (*far left*) are rich in nutrients and easy to find. Chickweed (*left*), along with waterweed, is a favorite water plant food that aquatic turtles enjoy eating.

MY PET

How Much Food?

A turtle that gets too much food becomes fat and suffers liver damage. In addition, its biological defenses and reproductive ability decline. You need to find out just how much food to give your pet.

The test begins:

Let your turtle fast for one day. The next day, weigh the quantity of fresh food that you want to serve. As soon as the creature slows down noticeably in its eating, determine how much it has eaten by subtracting the leftovers from the original amount. In the future, give the turtle only half the amount used in the experiment, and keep an eye on its weight.

My test results:

preference can change as the turtle grows, as indicated in the profiles.

The term *diet* has been specifically chosen. At first, most aquatic turtles give the impression that they are always hungry. They beg even though they are not hungry. That is the danger, because you could easily overfeed the turtle out of sympathy. Overfeeding can damage growth, especially with young creatures—which usually will grow too quickly—and lead to shell deformities. Both young and adult turtles quickly become too fat. With a carefully chosen diet, you avoid such mistakes. "Sticking to a diet" means nothing more than always serving the appropriate nutrients in the right amounts.

Unbeatable: A Diet from Nature

Natural food is fresh, varied, tasty, and naturally filled with all essential vitamins and trace elements. This type of feeding is heartily recommended.

Sources for this Land of Milk and Honey:

▶ You can cultivate waterweed, hornwort, and aquatic snails in your backyard pond.
▶ You can get crickets and young grasshoppers in pet shops. It is also easy to breed these creatures at home, as long as you can keep them from getting out of their enclosure.
▶ Mosquito larvae will appear spontaneously in basins of rainwater

outdoors. Simply fish them out.

- You can also catch food animals with a net in other bodies of water. Just make sure there are no regulations against collecting food creatures.
- You can get *Enchytraeidae* (small relatives of earthworms) and tubifex worms year-round in pet shops. Because of their lifestyle (they live in the mud on the bottom of flowing waters), these red annelid mud worms are usually severely contaminated with heavy metals. So buy only well-watered ones from a pet shop.
- In your yard, you can find slugs and snails of all types, earthworms, millipedes, isopods, and grubs. These small creatures are a natural component in a well-managed compost pile, especially if you set it up in such a way that it offers the desired creatures shelter and food.
- As a substitute for the uncommon grubs, pet shops sell live mealworms and darkling beetle larvae. Since they are low in fat and vitamins, you should feed these only once a day and one at a time to give your turtle something to do. They should never be used as the foundation for a diet.

Food from Reserves

This type of food will be necessary any time you cannot go "hunting" for fresh food. The advantage of this basic program from the pet shop is its easy availability. All you have to do is buy the food and divide it up. So if you cannot easily catch the small food animals live, get some other species in freeze-dried or frozen form. As long as the quality is good, their nutritional value is nearly comparable to the live versions.

You can get freeze-dried crustaceans (freshwater shrimp and water fleas), insects, and insect larvae (as a mix). Tubifex, red and white mosquito larvae, and water fleas are available frozen. For larger appetites, whole freshwater fish and newborn mice are good choices.

Of course, frozen products should be thawed a portion at a time and served at either room or water temperature. **Note:** Food that is dried in the sun or the air is not equivalent to freeze-dried

---

The nutritional value of snails is quite low, but they provide calcium through their shells.

or frozen food because some nutritional elements and vitamins are lost in the process. This type of food is rarely available in stores, but you still should check the information provided by the manufacturer.

Commercially Manufactured Foods for Turtles

You can also purchase commercially manufactured foods in pet shops. It is formulated generically—that is, to be appropriate for many species. It may not correspond precisely to the dietary recommendations shown in this book.

For omnivores and pure carnivores, this food consists of a mixture of chopped-up freshwater shrimp, mollusks, insects, and animal by-products in the form of an extrudate. It has a protein content of around 40 to 50 percent and a fat content of 4 to 5 percent. If you do not find any information about the proportions of calcium and phosphorus, then use this mix only in very small amounts for dieting days to give the turtle something to do and certainly not as a sole source of food for raising young turtles or for adult animals.

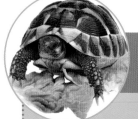

SPECIAL CONSIDERATIONS FOR FEEDING TURTLES

	When to Feed?	What to Feed?
Young tortoises	Daily for the first 2 to 3 years; the food must always be accessible.	Fresh food on the ground, hay in a pile must always be available.
Female tortoises in the mating season and up to one month after laying eggs	Feed several times a day in portion sizes that are quickly consumed so they do not go bad.	Select fresh food with high protein content and extra calcium; also cuttlefish bone.
Young aquatic turtles	Fresh food daily; the food must always be in the water so it is eaten before it goes bad.	Freshwater shrimp, water fleas, insects and insect larvae, and *Enchytraeus* worms (live or freeze-dried).
Growing aquatic turtles	Twice a day during active times; live food must not die before being eaten; 2 days of fasting per week.	About 60% of total amount as for young animals, 40% in the form of whole (dead) ornamental and bait fish.

For omnivores, you can always supplement the recommended portion of frozen or freeze-dried animal protein with fresh green food.

Pure carnivores can be given a portion of their food in fresh form, such as freshwater fish or fresh beef heart, plus calcium supplements.

Food Supplements for All Turtle Species

Lime: Always keep lime available, preferably in the form of a cuttlefish shell (from pet shops), which your turtle can nibble at will. The need for lime is particularly high in young turtles and in females during the egg-laying phase.

Vitamins: If your turtle gets fresh (live) food and UV light and it lives outdoors in the summer, supplementary vitamins are not necessary. Provide vitamins only after consultation with a veterinarian.

Trace elements: As with vitamins, these should be unnecessary if your turtle is kept outdoors and eats a natural diet. Here, too, provide trace elements only in accordance with your veterinarian's recommendations.

If you're not sure what food supplements your particular turtle should receive, it's best not to give it anything until you've made a thorough investigation of the issue. Giving the wrong supplements could do harm to your pet.

CHECKLIST

Who Eats What?

The nutritional needs of turtles can change. You will find information about the best way to feed them in the Profiles.

○ Tortoises are happy for their whole lives with a plant diet that always contains the right 1.5:1 to 2:1 ratio of calcium and phosphorus.

○ Young aquatic turtles are practically pure carnivores as long as they live in the water.

○ The food preference of aquatic turtles may change with age.

○ Species of aquatic turtles that prefer to live on land generally eat a mixed diet. Examples include the Eastern Box Turtle and the Amboina Box Turtle.

○ Aquatic turtle species that live in the water often get most of their food from protein. Examples of purely carnivorous turtles are the Musk Turtle and Snake-necked Turtle.

○ Many aquatic turtles also get most of their food from plants. Examples include certain species of Sliders.

Preparing Homemade Foods

Is the daily cutting up of food for your carnivore too much work?
Here is how to make your job easier. A single food preparation process can give
you a turtle food aspic that can be kept in the freezer for up to six months.

IN THE EARLY 1970s, the turtles in the Frankfurt, Germany, zoo were being given food in aspic form. It contained all necessary ingredients. No one knows who was the first person to get this bright idea for the food. We should erect a monument to this person. There are also many recipes in published sources.

Aspic Food

The mixture recommended here is based on the scientifically formulated original recipe and is intentionally kept simple. It contains everything that an aquatic turtle needs for healthy nutrition. With ingredients such as squid, mussels, and fresh shrimp, you can vary the taste and make the food more varied and interesting for the turtle.

When you make this food into an aspic, in a single work session you can prepare turtle food for 3 to 6 months, which even a substitute caregiver can comfortably serve. You should not store the mixture for more than 6 months for reasons of proper food handling.

Ingredients for the Basic Recipe

You need the following ingredients:
- 1 lb. (400 g) whole freshwater fish
- ½ lb. (200 g) heart,
- ½ lb. (200 g) squid in natural state,
- ¾ lb. (300 g) shrimp or krill (in meal form, 50% protein, feed store),
- 2 eggs with shell (raw),
- plus shells from two eggs (raw or boiled) or half a cuttlebone as a source of calcium,
- up to ½ lb. (200 g) of greens— depending on the turtle's dietary requirements, young leaves of stinging nettle; arugula; clover; chickweed; carrots; apples; unhusked, boiled rice or grits,
- high-quality food gelatin (from food store), and
- vitamin and mineral additives (from a veterinarian).

TIP

Serve bite-sized pieces

Aquatic turtles have lots of trouble with large pieces of food. Strands get torn off and contaminate the water. So cut up the food into bite-sized pieces. This will produce less waste. Suck up any waste from the water immediately, for it quickly goes bad. Remember to remove waste from inside the filter or it will recirculate toxic materials into the aquarium.

How to proceed: All ingredients are washed thoroughly under running water. Then puree the protein with a little water in a high-speed mixer (blender) until you get a liquid broth with a consistency similar to honey. Do the same with the remaining ingredients.

Mix everything thoroughly and heat to 176°F (80°C) (check it with a thermometer). As you continue stirring, let the mixture cool down to 122° to 140°F (50° to 60°C). Add high-quality

process, so it's best to prepare a lot of food at one time. This way, you can freeze the extra food and use it as needed over a period of time.

For omnivorous aquatic turtles, use the aspic only as a supplement while you feed fresh herbaceous material every day. If the turtles are primarily herbaceous, they get 60 to 80 percent plant material. This can consist of water

DID YOU KNOW THAT . . .

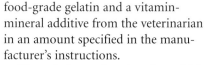

. . . in the wild, tortoises eat surprisingly little food?

This fact came from scientific studies when the daily food amount of a 2.2-pound (1 kg) Red-footed Tortoise was ascertained. The creature ate around ⅓ ounce (10 g) of fresh clover, about a handful, and was still totally healthy. This is interesting since you now know that your pet is not really starving if it temporarily eats less than usual.

food-grade gelatin and a vitamin-mineral additive from the veterinarian in an amount specified in the manufacturer's instructions.

The gelatin needs to be of very high quality. Otherwise, the food will not be solid enough and will come apart in the warm water much too quickly.

Pour the preparation into a baking pan to solidify, and cut the mass into appropriately sized daily rations. Now these can be frozen in plastic bags and thawed easily as needed. Preparing food for turtles can be a time-consuming

plants, e.g., from the backyard pond and/or tender plants such as chickweed.

Breeding Live Food for Aquatic Turtles

Catching food animals from the wild was explained earlier. You can also breed high-quality live food at home with minimal expense.

Breeding Earthworms
Earthworms have a high calcium content (about 0.7 percent in dry

mass). The common earthworm (*Lumbricus terrestris*) and night crawler can be found in loamy soils. The red-brown *Lumbricus rubellus* and the smaller *Lumbricus castaneus* live in humus.

Getting started: Use a simple wood box like a large fruit box or a small cement tub from a hardware store. Fill this

It is exciting to breed brine shrimp. **Children are fascinated** by their appearance out of "nowhere."

loosely three-quarters full with loam or humus. Now collect some earthworms by digging in the soil, and put them into the box. Put some coarse cloth over the box to darken it. That will allow in air. The worms, which do not like sunlight, will stay closer to the surface, which makes them easier to take out later. The appropriate temperature is 59° to 77°F (15° to 25°C).

Keep the soil slightly damp, never wet. Put in some spoiled, untreated lettuce, fruit, and vegetable garbage. The better the variety and the quality, the better the worms are for the turtle later. When it is nearly all gone after a week or two, put in some more food.

How to feed an earthworm to a turtle: Hold it out to the turtle with fairly long feeding tweezers. Do not throw the worm into the water, or it will die quite quickly if it is not eaten immediately.

Breeding Brine Shrimp

Since brine shrimp (*Artemia salina*) are fed with green algae, they are very rich in vitamins.

Getting started: Fill an aquarium with a capacity of 3-gallons (10 L) half-full with tap water, into which you dissolve around 2 ounces (50 g) of kitchen salt per quart (liter). Put the container into the light at 77° to 86°F (25° to 30°C), either near a window or in bright sunlight. Put in a bag of live, adult brine shrimp (from a pet shop). Feed them according to instructions with the readily available microalgae *Nonnochlorosis*.

This is the only algae I can recommend, for I have not had good experiences with substitute foods.

Gentle aeration like that used in aquariums keeps the water in motion and the plankton in suspension.

Soon you will find tiny brown eggs on the bottom, from which the first larvae (nauplii) hatch after about 36 hours. They too eat the algae.

When you begin breeding with artemia eggs, you should get a small package that will soon be used up, because as time goes by, the hatching rate declines.

Note: The bottles with microalgae that you can get in stores will keep for only a limited time. So put the contents into an ice cube tray, freeze it, and store it frozen.

How to feed brine shrimp to a turtle: Use a coarse-mesh aquarium net to fish out a couple of adult artemia. Let them swim around in the water inside the turtle's enclosure.

Remember that the creatures will survive only for about an hour in freshwater. Feed them in limited numbers so that your turtle can catch them while they are still alive.

HEALTHY FOODS FOR YOUR TURTLE

	Healthy	Best to Avoid
For tortoises	Freshly cut herbs, unsprayed	Grass from the edge of the road, where cars and dogs have left "residue"
	Fresh-smelling hay cut before the bloom, as a supplement	Only commercial turtle food as main or sole nutritional source
	Vitamin-rich vegetable sprouts grown at home	Commercially prepared vitamins in droplet form (if necessary, only in consultation with a vet)
	Fruit of all kinds, but not sprayed, up to 10 percent of total food amount	Very sweet fruits (strawberries, bananas) amounting to more than 10 percent of the total food amount
	Select lettuce, wild herbs, and vegetables with a higher calcium than phosphorus content; for females developing eggs, watch protein content	Lettuce and vegetables with an excess of phosphorus or a high oxalic acid content (rhubarb, sorrel); plants that you do not recognize could be poisonous, do not feed them
For aquatic turtles	For omnivores, water plants of all types and tender herbs from the countryside	Complete replacement of fresh food with dry food
	Fresh food from nature, breeder, or pet store as food base	Only commercial food as the sole food source
	Calcium supplements in feeding insects and fresh water fish (to balance the excess of phosphorus)	Commercial foods if you do not know the calcium-phosphorus ratio and the fat content

2 **Commercially prepared tidbits** can be given occasionally and irregularly—they provide welcome variety for an aquatic turtle and give the creature something to do.

1 **Fruit** will be a treat for the turtle in the outdoor pen. It should not exceed 10 percent of the daily ration though.

3 **Insect larvae** are a "busy food" that you should give your pet only occasionally.

Breeding Snails

Because of their shell, snails are an outstanding source of calcium.

Getting started with water snails: Appropriate species come from the mud, plate, killer, bubble, and river snail families.

Put a 10- to 16-gallon (40 to 60 L) aquarium by a window, and fill it two-thirds full of water (the snails will use the available glass rim for laying eggs). Heating and lighting are not needed. Plant the aquarium with lots of egeria. Put in a pinch of fish food flakes, and let them go bad. Very soon, a green layer of algae will appear on the glass. Now you can put in 6 to 12 snails of one species (from a pet store). Depending on the family, they will either graze the layer of algae off the glass or look for loose material on the surface and on the bottom. The snails are fed with flakes or tablets.

Getting started with *Achatina* snails: These large, tropical land snails from the genus *Achatina* can be successfully bred at 79° to 82°F (26° to 28°C) and fed as young food animals.

Breeding takes place using unspoiled fruit and vegetable scraps in a terrarium with a bottom filled with forest dirt and leaves to a depth of 4 inches (10 cm). The terrarium should be kept continually moist because the snails hatch their young in tropical rain forests.

How to feed a snail to a turtle: Feed only young snails with a shell length of ¾ to 1½ inches (2 to 4 cm). Feed them one at a time, and with the shell. *Achatina* snails are land snails, so they should be eaten right away so they do not suffer and drown.

Breeding Crickets

Insects from the species *Acheta domestica* contain a great deal of protein (around 70 percent) and lots of calcium.

Getting started: Crickets can be bred at room temperature but breed more quickly at 77° to 86°F (25 to 30°C) in a 5-gallon (20 L) glass aquarium. Place the aquarium in a dark corner of the room, and put several layers of newspaper on the bottom. The papers will need to be changed regularly. Now fill the glass container about a third full with egg cartons and cardboard tubes (for hiding places). The aquarium does not need to be covered. The creatures cannot climb up the slippery walls. For food, the insects get fresh, unsprayed lettuce, fruit, and vegetable scraps, which are replaced daily when they go bad. Also put a couple of hazelnuts and dried figs (very high in calcium) plus a cuttlebone into the aquarium to improve the balance of calcium and phosphorus in the crickets by means of their food.

So that the crickets will lay eggs, put into the aquarium some empty 8-ounce (240 mL) cottage cheese containers filled to the brim with a mixture of sand and finely strained peat (in equal proportions). Keep the peat-sand mixture constantly moist. The young creatures will hatch after around 10 days. They will be sexually mature after 50 or 60 days.

Note: Males chirp to attract females. So make sure a male does not get out and hide behind the bureau. The sound could get quite loud at night.

How to feed a cricket to a turtle: Use both hands to cover both ends of one of the cardboard tubes in which crickets are hiding, lift it out of the breeding aquarium, and let the crickets fall into the water one by one for the turtle. You can also presort the crickets by shaking them into a mixing bowl, taking out only the largest ones by hand, and

> You can increase the value of **live food insects** when you feed them foods rich in minerals.

giving them to the turtle. The turtle should eat the crickets right away so they do not suffer and drown.

Breeding Japanese Water Fleas

The fleas are very good for raising freshly hatched aquatic turtles and for keeping adult turtles occupied. In contrast to indigenous water fleas, Japanese water fleas will spontaneously reproduce at room temperature. You can get information about how to begin from a pet shop or from ads in aquarium magazines.

Sprouting Seeds

Because of their high vitamin, mineral, and fiber content, sprouts are a good supplementary food. You can also get detailed information about sprouts in stores that sell them (health and natural food stores).

Questions About
Proper Nutrition

? How often should I feed my aquatic turtle?

Feed aquatic turtles amounts and combinations that vary on a daily basis. Young turtles should get tiny treats distributed throughout the day, such as water fleas. As the turtles grow older, feed them only once or twice a day. Build in some fasting days, on which you serve only a crumb of commercial food or a couple of water fleas. Then the following day, you can feed the turtle a newborn mouse. (The amount of food also changes in the wild.) Sexually mature females should be fed a variety of foods every day during the egg formation period and up to a month after the season's last clutch of eggs.

? Should my tortoise get the same food year-round?

Except during the rest times, tortoises continually get food in the form of fresh hay, which must always be available. From the spring through the summer, the hay is supplementary feed, and thereafter until the fall, it is the basic food. In other words, you reduce the fresh food by 50 to 70 percent so that your tortoise eats primarily hay.

Tortoises from tropical regions continually get the same type of fresh food. However, hay must always be available.

? Do I have to feed my tortoise at specific times?

Feed only during the times when your tortoise is active. That way, it will get the major portion (60 to 70 percent) in the early morning and then the remaining 30 to 40 percent at midday. If you offer the food during the rest periods, you disturb the turtle in its natural daily rhythm, or else it eats the food later after the food may have gone bad.

? How do I put together a food that is rich in vitamins?

Sprouted seeds are a natural source of vitamins that complement the daily food well. In brief, here are the necessary steps. Fill a jelly or honey jar with 1 to 2 tablespoons (15 to 30 mL) of viable seeds so that they are loosely distributed on the bottom of the jar. Soak the seeds according to instructions, rinse well, and let drain. Close the jar with muslin or gauze held in place with a rubber band. Place the jar at an angle on a ½ inch (1 cm) wedge (e.g., cork) so that the seeds lie side by side. Initially, the seeds sprout in the dark. Thereafter, keep them in a bright but not sunny place at 64° to 70°F (18° to 21°C). Until harvest time, spray daily with lukewarm water and let them drain. Let wheat for food purposes (tortoises, crickets) grow into a thick, green lawn about 4 inches (10 cm)

long. Serve sunflowers and cress as soon the first green sprouts appear and the others once they reach a little over 1 inch (3 cm).

? Why do the water fleas die a few minutes after I put them into the aquarium?

When feeding live water fleas, you can avoid many disappointments if you observe a few tricks. Indigenous water fleas in the wild prefer temperatures under 64°F (18°C) and need a high oxygen content in the water. Your turtle presumably lives in water that is 75° to 79°F (24° to 26°C). That is a difference of up to 15°F (8°C) for the water fleas. They die either right away from shock or more slowly through oxygen starvation (warm water always contains less oxygen than cold). So shortly before you feed the water fleas, slowly bring them up to the temperature in the aquarium. That way, they will survive for at least a half hour. They will be eaten up by then, anyway. Instead of indigenous water fleas, you can also use Japanese water fleas.

? What is "meadow plankton," and how do I gather it?

The term *meadow plankton* is used to lump together all the insects living in a field, for example. In order to gather meadow plankton, you need a standard plankton or butterfly net. Sweep it vigorously over the tips of the grass in a meadow. You will find bugs, moths, and grasshoppers in the net. Use a jelly jar with a few stems of grass for the creatures to hold on to, and bring the valuable food to your turtle. Do not forget to put some air holes in the lid. You can make these from the inside with an awl or a hammer and nail by placing the lid upside down on a piece of wood.

Important note: you must never gather meadow plankton in nature preserves. Take only as much as you can feed live immediately. The creatures suffer inside the jar away from their accustomed habitat.

? What is the story on the quality of live food animals?

Food animals from the wild are filled with nutrients that they have ingested. When you breed them—crickets, for example—the quality of the insects depends on the food you give them. A variety of vegetables and wild herbs in unsprayed condition are thus much better than a "diet" of bran and oatmeal. The nutrients are passed on directly to the turtle since they are inside the bodies of the food animals.

Well Cared for and Healthy

Your commitment to care is a crucial factor in your turtle's well-being. The more you put into it, the better things will be for the armored pet in your house.

Proper Care

If you observe your turtle attentively and inspect the setup regularly, you will quickly get a sense of what kinds of care are required. That way, you effectively assure your animal's health and well-being.

YOUR TURTLE gets the best care when you consider and adapt the recommendations in this book. A liberal calculation of how much space to provide, well-ordered temperature changes, and lighting adjusted to the needs of the species amount to half the battle. It is also important for the turtle to be able to live out its individual daily and yearly rhythm and get a balanced selection of foods. That way, it will remain vital for many years and develop into a healthy animal.

Keeping an Eye on the Turtle

Despite the greatest care, your turtle may one day get worms or become sick. You should check your animal's health regularly and consult with a vet if necessary.
Daily: During the active period, check if your turtle exhibits normal behavior or any injuries.
Weekly: Pick up the turtle and check the bottom shell, the deep folds in the skin, and the vent to be sure they are free of damage and are clean. Also examine the eyes and mouth, and listen for any breathing noises.

Once a month: Weigh your turtle, and write down the weight.
Once a year: Have the veterinarian check a sample of the droppings and the turtle itself at the end of August. You should have this health check done routinely before hibernation. Early examination is important so that your turtle can get treatment before hibernation, if necessary. Don't ignore your pet's health requirements, as doing so could lead to serious problems.

On hot days, turtles look for a shady place where they can cool off.

You can train replacement caregivers if they can
watch what you do for a couple of days
and feed the turtle themselves.

Proper Terrarium Care with Tortoises

Perfect hygiene inside the terrarium is just one of the many important aspects of providing care. This involves a couple of tasks.

Daily: Remove droppings and leftover food. Scrub the water bowl with hot water, a brush, and unscented cleanser. The scents in cleaning products are a serious bother to the turtle's sensitive nose—even if you think you have rinsed the bowl thoroughly.

Every two weeks: Wet patches of dirt between the water bowl and the land are a breeding ground for worm eggs and larvae. They survive for a long time in the warm, moist environment and continue multiplying. So every two weeks, use a tablespoon to dig out these areas and put in fresh sand. Take care of the microclimate in the setup so that your turtle can always find comfortable

If you know your pet well, a quick glance will tell you if your turtle is in perfect health.

areas that meet its current need for damp or dry ground or for warmer and cooler areas. You can assure these conditions by regularly watering the plants or moistening the digging area. You should follow the recommendations for each species in the Profiles section of this handbook.

Proper Care for a Setup on the Balcony or in the Yard

Daily: Sweep out the setup on the balcony, in the cold frame, or in the greenhouse, and remove leftover food and droppings. Treat the food, water dishes, and the wormy dirt as described in the section about how to care for a terrarium. Also make sure to check the walls of the setup to be sure they can contain the turtle. A root tipped at an angle can be used as a climbing aid, allowing your protégé to get out. In the summer, remove fruits from the bottom since they can ferment or get moldy.

Once a year: Renew the turtle's preferred toilet area in the outdoor pen to a depth of about 3 inches (7 cm). Alternatively, you could also heat the area with a propane torch, rake it up 2 or 3 times, and heat it up again. (Be sure you follow safety precautions when you do this.) That way, you reliably kill all the worm eggs and larvae.

In May or June, cut back the shrubbery in the enclosure. In November, empty the pond with a dirty water pump while you simultaneously stir up the decayed matter. Finally, put in freshwater. Leaves generally collect on one side of the shore, where you can remove them. You do not have to worry about the small animal life in the pond any more; your turtle has already taken care of that for you during the summer.

Aquatic Turtles — Proper Aquarium Care

Daily: Remove droppings and leftover food. You will rarely find the droppings in solid form. However, crumbled fibers and pieces collect either in the filter or as decayed matter on the bottom of the aquarium. You can use a hose to siphon off the decayed material. For hygienic reasons, do not use your mouth to suck out the water. Rather, fill the hose with aquarium water by putting one end in the tank and stopping the other end with your thumb. Hold this end of the hose in a bucket placed lower than the water level in the aquarium, and then release your thumb. The water will flow out of the tank and into the bucket. Once a week: Filter pads must be rinsed regularly. Small pieces of food and droppings dissolve within 3 to 5 days, depending on size and composition, through the action of bacteria in the water. If these residues get the upper hand, the bacteria that utilize the waste multiply to the extent that you can see them as a milky clouding of the water. Now it is definitely time for a complete water change.

CHECKLIST

Preparing for Vacation

Look for a competent individual to take care of your turtle. Contacting local terrarium clubs may help. Give your vacation substitute the Pet Sitter's Guide.

○ Check the thermometer and hygrometer readings for the correct values. Make sure the filter is working properly. Check to be sure that the spotlight gets turned on and off at the programmed times.

○ Show the individual the fuses that control the setup and the circuit breaker. Have replacement bulbs available.

○ Prepare the necessary food supplies (aspic food, hay, commercial food). Specify the amounts and times for feeding.

○ Explain the turtle's normal behavior. Factor in any peculiarities, such as courtship display, egg laying, and initial signs of hibernation.

○ Make sure to leave the vet's address and phone number so that the substitute can get help in any emergency.

○ Ideally, the substitute will provide all care and feeding in accordance with the specifications in this book.

Turtles in Hibernation

Our children love their turtles, and it is touching to see how they take care of them. When it is time for Paul and Pauline—two Sliders—to hibernate, our children are very insecure about leaving them for so long in the cold and without food. What is the best way to explain hibernation to the children?

CHILDREN ARE NOT THE ONLY ONES who find it stressful to get the turtles ready for hibernation. It takes some willpower for many adults turtle owners to forego suddenly the daily concern for the right water and air temperature and for preparing a balanced diet.

Patient Explanation for the Children

Explain to the children symbolically, when they are 10 to 12 years old, that it is colder in the bedroom than in the living room. Explain that when people are asleep, they usually experience neither hunger nor thirst. It is the same with the turtle, except that its "sleep" in the winter lasts longer. This happens because in the wild, the turtle would find nothing to eat under the ice and snow. It thus sleeps through to spring.

Hibernation for Advanced Turtle Enthusiasts

If your children are older, explain the scientific facts: turtles are cold-blooded creatures that cannot produce their own body warmth. Their body thus cools off to the same extent as the surrounding temperature. Species whose natural habitat lies outside the subtropical regions survive during this time by withdrawing into a protected spot and drastically reducing their metabolism. Breathing, heart rate, and movement are reduced to a minimum.

A Totally Natural Process

The decreasing length of days triggers the hibernation impulse. That is why daylight is so important. The shortening days control the turtle's inner clock and produce a hormonal change that reduces metabolism, halts food intake, and empties the intestine. It would be harmful to the creature if you were to attempt to prevent hibernation through warming and feeding. Once the turtle has dug into its hibernation spot, the rising temperature in the spring will provide the wakeup call. So for the turtle, before the end of March to April, there should be no more than 3 to 5 days that are warmer than 54° to 59°F (12° to 15°C). This happens frequently as early as February, though, if the hibernation box with the turtle is stored in the garage, tool shed, or attic. Waking up and getting cooled back down after a couple of days really costs the turtle a lot of energy.

With more experience, you will recognize a deterioration of the water quality early by a slight cloudiness. That is the right time to do a partial water change. A good test for cloudy water is the beam from a flashlight. In the dark, the beam of light shows up very clearly in the water. If this is the case, change the water right away. Also clean the filter material with clear water only so that the beneficial little life-forms that live on it and process the water escape harm. Once a month: Generally, you should change the aquarium water once a month—less frequently if the water is not so dirty. At the same time, this is a good opportunity to rinse the decayed material out of the corners and from the bottom. Also carefully clean all roots and glass panes with a sponge. The dirt will run out with the draining water. Rinse with clear water, and let it run out too.

Your turtle can spend the exciting time of the water change in a bucket or a quarantine terrarium. Before you put the turtle back into the aquarium, bring the new water up to the same temperature that you previously measured in the old water.

Note: Bogwood and peat extracts sometimes produce a light coloration that is totally harmless. They are even advantageous to turtles that like things to be in the dark. Dirt from the land portion that a digging turtle flings into the water can also produce a milky discoloration. This too is harmless.

Like all aquatic turtles, the Musk Turtle *is grateful for water quality that continually remains high.*

Hibernation for Turtles

Like estivation, hibernation is a genetically programmed survival strategy
for many turtle species. It must never be interfered with.
In fact, it requires careful preparation.

IF THE NATURAL HABITAT of
your turtle is in the temperate
latitudes, hibernation is a good
strategy for surviving the cold
season. The turtle can simply ride out
the time of low temperatures and lack
of food while it sleeps. Since it is a cold-
blooded creature that cannot regulate
its own body warmth, it cools down to
the same degree as the surrounding
temperature.

Important Preparations

In order for your turtle to make it
through the winter and wake up fit and
healthy the following spring, you need
to take a few precautions.

TIP

Continuous checks during the winter

Most damage during hibernation is the result
of wintering a sick or worm-infested turtle as
well as either an excessively dry or wet
environment. So early worming and a health
check at the end of August are as essential as
ongoing hygrometer checks in the winter
quarters.

Making a Hibernation Box for a Tortoise

When you build a hibernation box, you
closely duplicate the natural conditions
inside a dirt hiding place. The rising of
water through capillary action from the
layer of damp expanded clay keeps the
hibernation environment at 80 to 90
percent humidity so that your turtle can
neither dry out nor become drenched.
Size: For the container, you need a
wooden box with a surface area of
around 28 × 28 inches (70 × 70 cm) and
a height of 32 inches (80 cm). There is
no harm in using a larger box. However,
if it is significantly smaller or lower, the
turtle can become dehydrated more
easily.
Filling: Cover the bottom with a piece
of pond liner that comes up about ½
inch (1 cm) high to form a basin. Put in
a 4-inch (10 cm) layer of expanded clay,
and add a plastic pipe about 35 inches
(90 cm) long. The pipe, through which
you can pour in water as needed, goes
to the basin made of pond liner. Cover
the expanded clay with a root barrier
(from a gardening supply store) to keep
the turtle out. On top of that comes an
8-inch (20 cm) layer of dirt that you
compress lightly by hand. The rest of
the box is filled with beech leaves. Put a
hygrometer (calibrate it every year!) in
the place where the turtle normally

When fall comes, many turtles focus on the search for an appropriate place to spend the winter.

hibernates, at the border between dirt and leaves. It is protected by a plastic cup and must be at a humidity of 80 to 90 percent (however, *Testudo horsfieldii* hibernates at a humidity of 65 percent). If the humidity is too low, put in about 3½ ounces (100 mL) of water, and wait two days. Then measure the humidity again.

Note: Under no circumstances should the turtle itself or the place where it lies be moistened directly.

Making a Hibernation Basin for Aquatic Turtles

If your turtle hibernates on the bottom of a body of water in the wild, it will want an underwater resting place. The best way to provide this is in the form of a cement basin placed into an unheated cellar or a greenhouse. Put enough water into the basin so that

while the creature is on the bottom, it can get air without having to swim. You can create a secure spot by imitating the decayed material of a natural body of water with floating foam peanuts about 1 inch (3 cm) long. Cover 95 percent of the cement basin with a board to keep out the light. If the turtle is still restless, close the lid entirely.

If your aquatic turtle wants to hibernate on land, it will climb up onto the land portion in search of a spot. Place the turtle into a hibernation box of the type described for tortoises. A slightly moist mixture of deciduous leaf litter and bark mulch in equal proportions keeps the humidity at around 90 percent.

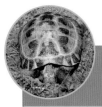

APPROPRIATE PLACES FOR HIBERNATION

WHERE	ADVANTAGES	DISADVANTAGES
Vaulted cellar	Constant temperature and humidity around 90%	Rarely found in rural areas
House cellar	Available in nearly every home, easy to keep dark	Modern cellars have dry air, temperature rarely below 54°F (12°C); supervision required
Window bay/cellar window	Capillary moisture reduces drying out in winter quarters; easy visual check	Usable only on north side because sunny window bays warm up too early in the year
Refrigerator	Temperature can be controlled precisely; easy access to animal	Dries out tortoises; electrical energy is expensive
Greenhouse	Natural (shorter) hibernation time and winter quarters in potting soil are possible	Not appropriate for *Testudo horsfieldii* species, which should hibernate for 7 months

A Hibernation Box in the Refrigerator

Tortoises: Your tortoise can spend the winter in the vegetable drawer of the refrigerator instead of in the cellar. Fill a transparent container with bark mulch or beech leaves, and bury the tortoise in them—right side up, of course. The container can be the size of a shoe box or larger. A commonly available box with a lid is a good choice. With boxes that have airtight lids, put some holes into the sidewalls and the top with a $\frac{5}{16}$ inch (8 mm) drill—one hole about every 2 to 3 inches (6 to 7 cm). Tape a hygrometer into place inside the container so that you can read it easily from the outside. By using a damp sponge the size of a matchbox, which you tape under the lid—and which must never touch the turtle—you can keep the humidity at 80 to 90 percent. Make sure that nothing gets moldy.

Aquatic turtles: An aquatic turtle is put into a box with enough water to cover the shell by a $\frac{1}{2}$ inch (1 cm). For "land hibernation," the box is filled halfway with peat moss. The size of the box should allow the turtle to turn around in a circle effortlessly. It must not be able to reach the lid while standing up with neck extended. The turtle also needs this space for breathing air, even though its need is low during hibernation. Drill a few air holes in the sides above the water line, as described for tortoises. That way, the turtle can also spend the winter in the refrigerator.

Wintering in the Greenhouse

Tortoises: Set the hibernation box in the floor of the greenhouse in such a way that the lid is flush with the ground. The bottom of the box, the pond liner, the layer of expanded clay, and the root barrier are omitted. The bottom is replaced by soldered wire mesh (mesh size ⅜ inch/10 mm) or a concrete slab that will keep mice from getting in from below. Capillary moisture will still be able to rise inside the box, and any excess water can still seep out.

Fill the box with about 20 inches (50 cm) of bark mulch and the remainder up to the rim with beech leaves. As soon as your tortoise moves into the winter quarters on its own, cover the container with another piece of wire mesh (⅜ inch/10 mm mesh size) stretched over a wooden frame.

Aquatic turtles: Put in the previously described cement tub flush with the ground, but raise the bottom of the tub with cement slabs or foam mats so that your turtle can get air.

Inappropriate: Hibernating in the Yard or Pond

You always hear recommendations to let aquatic turtles hibernate in the backyard pond and tortoises in the yard. I advise against both of these. Even though certain turtles in areas where they naturally occur can handle this (e.g., in warm lowlands), doing this should be left to experts. For all other tortoise and aquatic turtle species, the spring and fall are too variable and cold for too long, in part due to global climate change. Numerous deaths continually confirm this.

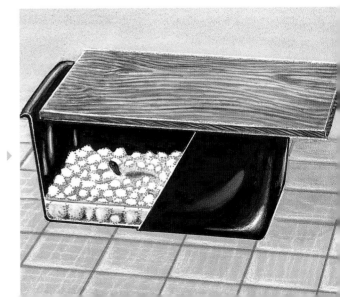

You can create effective and economical winter quarters for your aquatic turtle by setting it up comfortably with foam packing pellets and keeping it dark.

Is your turtle a candidate for a summer rest?

Many turtle species from hot, dry climates survive the foodless, life-threatening hot period in summer rest (also known as estivation). This test will point out the difference between that and an illness.

The test begins:

Keep regular records of your turtle's weight. If the creature becomes inactive and loses its appetite, you can easily determine if this behavior is a prelude to summer rest or the initial signs of an illness. In anticipation of the summer rest, the turtle eats less and less but in the end gains weight. On the other hand, a sick animal keeps losing weight even before it loses its appetite and becomes apathetic.

My test results:

Proper Hibernation

At the end of August, you should bring a fecal sample to the veterinarian and perhaps worm your turtle according to the veterinarian's instructions. There is still time to treat and cure an illness. Everything else a healthy turtle will take care of by itself.

The creature may still be walking around in October or November but without eating. This is the time to lower the air and/or water temperature gradually in the setup by 4° to 6°F (2° to 3°C) at a time every 3 to 5 days. That way, within 14 days, you will have lowered the temperature by a total of 20° to 24°F (10° to 12°C), so that the temperature inside the enclosure is around 59° to 63°F (15° to 17°C). During these 2 weeks, most turtle species will continue fasting, emptying their intestine, sticking their head into a dark corner, and waiting for winter. A turtle in a greenhouse will generally go into the box on its own without prompting from you, for you have no control over the decrease in temperature and the shortening of the days. If the tortoise does not empty its intestine—perhaps the living conditions are too dry—then bathe it daily for a half-hour in water at 77°F (25°C) until that happens. Under no circumstances must the creature hibernate with a full intestine. It would die from the inevitable decomposition of undigested food in its innards.

Checks and Water Care

Weigh your pet before hibernation, and write down its weight. You will need to inspect the turtle and the setup regularly during hibernation.

Aquatic turtles: Check the setup and the turtle once a week. If the water is clear, it does not need to be changed. However, if you notice a milky cloudiness, put the turtle into a different container, rinse off the foam pellets, and clean the basin with clear water. Before you put in fresh water, cool it to the proper temperature. Then put the turtle back in.

Tortoises: Because of the stable microclimate inside the box, you need to check only every 3 weeks. Weigh your tortoise, and make particularly sure that the hygrometer inside the box still displays the proper value.

The Right Temperature

Generally, your pet will hibernate at 39° to 43°F (4° to 6°C). Since not every winter has the same temperatures in the wild, your tortoise has developed a protection mechanism that allows it to survive for 3 to 4 days during temperature increases to 50° to 59°F (10° to 15°C), which can occasionally happen when the weather changes. This is referred to as a latency period. In other words, the creature can wake up for a short while and then return to hibernation without great energy expenditure when the weather turns cold again.

Note also the exceptions for turtle species that hibernate at a higher temperature (see "Profiles," pp. 22–31).

So do not fret if the temperature is not as cold in your cellar as you might like. Try to achieve the recommended temperature range for hibernation, but do not worry if you go over it. As long as your turtle remains dug in and quiet and loses no more than 10 percent of its weight, it can stay in the hibernation box even at higher temperatures. However, if the turtle climbs around on the leaves, it is awake. Now it must be transferred to the terrarium and taken care of.

The microclimate in the hibernation box is easy to control with the aid of the hygrometer inside it.

An Orderly Wakeup from Hibernation

Tortoises: A tortoise that spends the winter in the cellar comes out of hibernation in around early to late April. Then it sits around for a few days on the leaves.

Put the tortoise into its terrarium, and keep it at room temperature for 2 or 3 days. Then bathe it in a

into the setup at the same temperature. Every 2 days, raise the temperature of the air and water by a couple of degrees until you reach the normal temperature for the particular species.

After about a week, the turtle will begin to eat.

Refrigerator turtles: Release the turtle from the cold at the specified time (see "Profiles," pp. 22–31), and put it into the terrarium at room temperature. Now wait until it starts to walk around. Only now is the turtle totally awake,

DID YOU KNOW THAT ...

. . . many turtles can hibernate even in fairly warm temperatures?

The biologist Pawlowski had some species of turtle hibernate for several years at temperatures of 54° to 59°F (12° to 15°C), including *Emys orbicularis*, *Sternotherus odoratus*, *Trachemys scripta elegans*, and *Chinemys reevesii*. He kept the creatures separate and in the dark. After the hibernation, the turtles showed neither health problems nor significant weight loss.

physiological salt solution at 75°F (24°C). Now the temperature in the terrarium can be adjusted to the level recommended for the particular species. Give the tortoise fresh food every day. After about a week, it will begin to eat.

Aquatic turtles: They indicate the end of hibernation through increased activity. Bring the hibernation basin and the turtle into a bright room at 64° to 68°F (18° to 20°C), and remove the shade.

After 2 or 3 days, place the turtle

and you can plug in the heat and the spotlight for the setup. Bathe tortoises as previously described.

Greenhouse turtles: If your pet has spent the winter in the hibernation hollow in the greenhouse, it will generally wake up as early as February or March because of the heating effect from the sun rising higher in the sky. Now turn on the heat and lighting until the end of May so that your turtle can experience a "springtime in the temperate zone" (i.e., a Mediterranean climate).

Common Diseases

The best measures for countering illness involve consistent prevention. This is the result of perfect hygiene, healthy food, and attention to the light and temperature demands of your pet. That way, it will remain healthy.

IN ORDER to be continually aware of your pet's general health, you should observe the turtle attentively once a day. With this exercise, a quick glance will soon be enough to give you information about your pet's condition. At least once a week, you should check it in accordance with the information in the table on page 95.

Avoiding Mistakes Right from the Start

Sometimes inexperienced turtle owners make the mistake of getting a young animal that is sick. So make sure that you get your turtle from healthy stock. Imported creatures captured in the wild, especially the ones you bring back yourself from some vacation bazaar or flea market, are often so compromised in advance (dehydrated, half-starved, infested with worms) that they can experience health problems. When buying an adult turtle, the danger of an emerging skeletal disease is reduced or is easier to detect. However, even these turtles can suffer from infections, which may have been caused by previous serious mistakes in providing care.

Symptoms of Illness

(By Dr. Renate Keil, D.M.V.)
Describing the symptoms of illness will help you recognize alarm signals early so you can take your turtle to the vet in a timely fashion. Treatments should always follow the vet's advice.

Difficulty Breathing

Symptoms: The turtle stretches its neck out straight, opens its mouth, and makes peeping, groaning, or snoring sounds. It also lets its head sag in fatigue.
Possible causes: Lung infection, constipation, egg binding, distension in stomach or intestine, bladder stones or clumps of uric acid that interfere with emptying the anal bladder, or edema

> TIP
>
> ### Recognizing sick turtles at point of purchase
>
> Have an experienced turtle owner go with you when you buy your pet. You can locate one in a nearby terrarium club. Young turtles, in particular, that are raised improperly have skeletal deformities and infections that can be difficult for laypeople to detect.

from kidney or heart disease. Difficulty breathing can be a result of herpes.

Treatment: Under no circumstances should you warm up the creature! Otherwise, the increased metabolism could threaten its life. Take your turtle to the vet immediately. Before treatment, the animal will need to be x-rayed. A herpes infection is usually

Treating **illnesses** at home can make them worse. It is essential to consult a vet!

fatal to turtles, and oftentimes treatment is not possible. The only way to save the remaining turtles is through immediate quarantine, hygiene, and disinfection measures. Fungal and bacterial infections are possible secondary infections. Treatment requires the expertise of a vet.

Diarrhea

Symptoms and possible causes: Runny feces from improper feeding, infection from single-celled animals, worms, fungi, or bacterial pathogens.
Treatment for tortoises: If no blood is mixed in with the feces and the creature acts lively otherwise, the diarrhea is caused by diet. Eliminate fruit, reduce the amount of green food, and add 80 percent hay with some dry leaves. Instead of water, serve chamomile tea or black tea (let it steep for 10 minutes).
Treatment for aquatic turtles: In the water, detecting runny feces due to illness is difficult. In order to get a fecal

sample, temporarily place the turtle into a damp quarantine box with no water. Feed it sparingly with low-fiber food (e.g., earthworms).

If the condition does not improve in 2 to 3 days, the turtle must go to the vet. Take along a fresh fecal sample.

Change in Urine

Symptoms and causes: With most turtles, the urine consists of a clear, watery portion and a white, slimy blot. Altered urine is thick. In advanced stages of illness, the white slime spoor is absent. Later it contains small pebbles. The animal behaves more calmly than usual. Its joints, including the hind legs, swell.

The less the tortoise drinks, the more uric acid condenses in large crystals. The crystals harm the structure of the kidneys.

The result is infections. The performance of the kidneys decreases, and the uric acids that can no longer be excreted poison the creature. Bladder stones or gout are the painful consequence.

An aquatic turtle shows the same symptoms. You can evaluate its urine more effectively if you put it temporarily into a damp quarantine box with no water, where the urine cannot dissolve immediately and remains visible.
Treatment: Take the turtle to the veterinarian right away! By way of prevention, always have clean drinking water available in the swimming basin. That is where the sick animal will prefer to spend time and drink more water.

Of course, this preventive measure does not apply to aquatic turtles.

POSSIBLE EFFECTS OF IMPROPER CARE

Symptoms	Cause	Remedy
A hook forms on the tip of the upper part of the beak.	The beak does not get worn down and sharpened by hard food.	The vet can shorten the hook. Serve more fiber in the food, and make a cuttlebone available. Check the protein content of the food.
The tortoise's claws become too long and crooked.	Not enough opportunities for exercise; ground too smooth; no surfaces for climbing available to wear down the claws. Too much protein in the food also greatly accelerates claw growth.	Enlarge the enclosure and put in pieces of sandstone or rough bricks. Encourage exercise. Check the protein content of the food.
Young animals develop bumpy, soft shell.	Improper nutrition, usually because of excessive phosphorus and excessively warm living conditions.	Comply with food and temperature specifications.
A tortoise has persistent diarrhea.	Lack of roughage, often an excess of sugar in food.	Increase the amount of fiber in the food, cut back on fruits.
One of two turtles hardly eats, does not grow, and appears apathetic.	It is cowed by the more active turtle that eats well and is growing, and the former is under stress.	The two turtles must be separated and kept where they cannot see one another.
The turtle eats continually and more than one or two bites of dirt per day.	It may be trying to get minerals that it needs by eating dirt.	Check the food for mineral content and get advice from the veterinarian.

Lung Infection

Symptoms: With tortoises and aquatic turtles, difficulty breathing and uncharacteristically long stays beneath the spotlight. With an aquatic turtle, a swimming position tilted to one side.
Possible causes: Draft; with aquatic turtles, a temperature below the water temperature. Tortoises and aquatic turtles walk around on the floor inside the house and are exposed to draft.
Treatment: Only by a veterinarian and after an x-ray.
Note: Healthy, pregnant female tortoises and aquatic turtles bask in the sun a lot. They will lack the other symptoms of illness described here.

Swollen Eyes

Symptoms: The eyelids are swollen, and the eyes are shut.
Possible causes: Draft, foreign object, injuries, vitamin A deficiency. With aquatic turtles, water contaminated by bacteria.
Treatment: Only by a veterinarian.
Note: All vitamin preparations that contain vitamins A and D_3 must be administered in proportion to the turtle's body weight.

Swollen Eardrum

Symptoms: The eardrum (above the jaw joint, behind the eye) bulges outward to a certain extent (pea shaped).
Possible causes: Middle ear infection; internal pus deposit.
Treatment: Only by a veterinarian.

Soft Shell

Symptoms: The shell is soft and bleeds at the seams.
Possible causes: Improper nutrition, vitamin D_3 poisoning.
Treatment: Only by a veterinarian; UV radiation and doses of calcium. Do not keep on sand or gravel since they will be eaten to excess during the illness.

Shell Deformities

Symptoms: Sinking in of top shell or pyramid-shaped buckling of individual scutes, especially during growth.
Possible causes: Improper nutrition, especially with a young animal; vitamin D_3 deficiency.
Treatment: By veterinarian.

Skin Lesions

Causes: Swelling from injuries or fresh scars.
Possible causes: Bite wounds, usually on legs and around the throat, injuries around the vent due to mating and mating attempts.
Treatment: By veterinarian.

Significant Peeling of Skin

Symptoms: The top layer of skin usually comes off in large pieces on the throat and legs, blistering down to raw flesh. This is different from the normal peeling with many aquatic turtles (Sliders and Snake-necked Turtles), where only the epidermis peels with an intact, fresh, new outer layer appearing under it.
Possible causes: Often an overdose of vitamin A from vitamin preparations or an excessively high vitamin injection.
Treatment: By a veterinarian.

2 **A healthy aquatic turtle** always looks alert and attentive. In addition, it has sleek, colorful skin. With young creatures, it is particularly colorful.

1 **The shell** of a healthy turtle is suspended level over the ground and does not drag.

3 **With Sliders,** old layers of the shell and epidermis regularly peel off. This is no cause for concern.

Increased Restlessness in a Female, Especially with Aquatic Turtles on Land (Egg Binding)

Symptoms: The sexually mature female walks around restlessly all day (aquatic turtles on land) and may dig holes. It is not able to lay its eggs. In extreme cases, the heels of the hind feet are chafed raw. Further symptoms include difficulty breathing.
Possible causes: Physiological or anatomical reasons.
Treatment: By a veterinarian.

"Intestinal Prolapse"

Symptoms: An aquatic turtle drags behind it a (mostly) light pink, transparent membrane sac that protrudes from the vent.
Possible causes: With male aquatic turtles, this occurs regularly. This involves the penis, which should be retracted within no more than a half-hour, and it is not an illness. However, if the creature is a female or if either sex drags the tissue around longer than an hour, then contact the vet. With tortoises, you must not wait but treat this immediately by wrapping the tissue in moist gauze to keep it from drying out.
Treatment: By a veterinarian.

Questions About Winter and Summer Rest

? I have an adult Spotted Turtle that stops eating for 1 or 2 months starting in the fall. However, it remains mobile in the aquarium during the winter. Now I find out it is supposed to hibernate. Is this correct?

Many species are so widespread in the wild—such as the Spotted Turtle, from Canada to Florida, and the European Swamp Turtle, from central Europe to Africa—that predicting the need for hibernation is difficult. If you did not get your animal from a breeder who can supply information about it, you can do a test—by observing carefully. If the creature stops eating, lower the temperature in the terrarium over the course of several days to 59° to 64°F (15° to 18°C). Does the animal then calm down? If so, this is an indication that it wants to begin hibernating. If you are still in doubt, use a temperature gradient. Your pet will have a choice between cold and hot. If it chooses *cold*, get it ready for hibernation. If it chooses *warm*, have it checked by the vet to see why it is no longer eating.

? My Boettger's Tortoise disappeared in the yard to hibernate. I cannot find it. What harm can happen to it if I let it hibernate there?

First, you can use a dog to try to pick up the tortoise's scent and dig it up. Let the dog get the scent in the tortoise's hiding place or toilet area, and search under bushes and in other places. If you do not find your tortoise, it is in danger of being tracked by rats or martens (weasels) that will eat the defenseless creature. Frost is less harmful to the tortoise, even if it is not entirely buried. However, see if you can spot it in the yard on warm days in February or March and then immediately put it into its heated terrarium.

? Can I let my turtle hibernate outdoors? My cellar is too warm, and there is no room in my refrigerator.

The concrete window bay on the north or northeastern side of the cellar might be a good solution. It is protected from frost, and the natural capillary moisture in the ground will keep the creature from becoming dehydrated while hibernating in the bed of leaves. Cover the floor drain of the window bay with a piece of clay pot so it does not get plugged, and put in about 2 inches (5 cm) of dirt on the floor. Fill the rest with dry beech leaves. Cover it with a piece of wire mesh ($\frac{3}{16}$ inch/5 mm mesh) to keep out the mice and other animals.

I keep reading that the Russian Tortoise is particularly difficult to keep, especially with respect to hibernation. Why is it so sensitive?

Your tortoise is a child of the desert. In other words, it is perfectly adapted to surviving in a dry, hot climate with scant food but not to daylong rain and running around in the cold and wind in damp slush. Its body has never had to defend itself against cold in combination with dampness. As a result, it is highly vulnerable to living conditions and hibernation that do not take this into consideration. In its natural hibernation hollow, the humidity is probably around 8 percent because of ground moisture rising through capillary action, even in the desert.

As it breathes, it takes in moist air, which keeps the lungs from drying out. However, if it hibernates in an excessively damp area, it can get moldy inside and out because it has developed no defenses against mold spores.

My turtle woke up in the middle of its hibernation. What should I do?

Your turtle may become active earlier than anticipated during its hibernation and with no apparent cause. (A foreseeable reason would be something like a major, early warming of the hibernation spot.) In that case, terminate the hibernation and take your turtle to the veterinarian. It may be sick. If so, it will need to be brought back to health in the terrarium or aquarium according to the veterinarian's recommendations. Follow his or her advice closely if you must nurse your pet back to health.

I do not have a place for my turtle to hibernate. I have heard it said that this will not matter and that it could even be harmful to young creatures.

You can find hibernation possibilities at a regional terrarium club. You can also use a refrigerator as winter quarters. If you do not satisfy your turtle's wish to hibernate, its body will be missing a vitally important rest. It will not die. As time goes on, though, it will become more susceptible to illnesses and will not be able to reproduce. Young turtles hibernate just like adult ones. Because of their small size, they are at particular risk of dehydration. Only young turtles that hatch late in the fall can be allowed to hibernate briefly in the following year starting in February for 1 to 3 months.

Keeping Busy and Feeling Fine

Setting up the enclosure with a view to variety, plus solicitous care, will stimulate all the turtle's senses, keep it physically fit, and prevent unnecessary daily stress.

Living Conditions Like in the Wild

There is a huge difference between a well-cared-for turtle and a creature "kept in prison." Here you will learn what your turtle needs in order to feel nearly as free as it does in the wild.

FIRST, A RECOMMENDATION: your turtle is a wild animal whose internal clock is set to survive in the natural world. This means that every species has developed its own daily routine. So the Eastern Box Turtle, for example, is active in the twilight, rather than during the daytime, like the Boettger's Tortoise. Be sure to take this into account with feeding times and caretaking duties. Avoid disturbing your pet during its rest phases.

Living Close to Nature

Looking for food: In the wild, finding food is a time-consuming matter that lasts for hours. It requires ranging far and wide and also rummaging. It would be nice if you made it possible for your pet to continue doing this, at least on a small scale. This means that your turtle should be able to find food all around the pen during its active time by using all its physical abilities and senses. An aquatic turtle should be able to hunt live, small creatures. This keeps the circulatory system fit and the senses sharp. It is good training for the muscles, and the shell gets scoured clean by rubbing against obstacles.

Territory: In the wild, turtles search for a territory where they can find secure places to get away to and rest, good areas for basking in the sun and laying eggs, and—if necessary—protected places for hibernating. Meeting these needs inside the enclosure at your home should be possible.

You will rarely be able to offer all this in a living room terrarium. However, I know devotees who have set up a whole room of over a 100 square feet (12 sq m) for their pet, complete with scenery: large agaves and potted shrubbery imbedded between natural boulders under a floodlight.

The Red-bellied Short-necked Turtle *is a very good swimmer and spends little time on land.*

Most turtle owners cannot set up this type of enclosure, so keeping a turtle outdoors becomes a good alternative. The following pages advise you about how to care for your turtle properly and close to nature.

Letting the Turtle Behave Naturally

In the wild, a young turtle does everything possible to avoid falling prey to a predator. This behavior is instinctive from birth. As the turtle grows, its shell provides adequate protection. When threatened by a predator, the turtle instantly pulls into its bunker and waits until the danger has passed.

What does this mean for you? Indoors—just as outdoors—a young turtle will at first always be on guard. This means that at first, it will scarcely take advantage of your whole imaginatively conceived terrarium since it will instinctively stay under cover to avoid possible threats. Then it will prefer to stay in the hiding place and be happy when you put the food where it can be reached easily.

In an indoor terrarium, a turtle generally learns quickly that it can go about its territory completely and without danger. However, if it is put into an outdoor pen for the summer—into a totally new territory—the instinctive caution quickly returns, especially if a young turtle may also be attacked there by cats, crows, or birds of prey. Even if you cover the enclosure with a bird net, your pet will often not totally put aside its innate alertness and shyness. If you understand this behavior on the part of the young turtle, you will not try to force behaviors of which it is not yet capable. As the turtle grows, it learns that there are no dangers to fear. In addition, because of its strong shell, it instinctively feels more secure—with the result that it will use a large outdoor enclosure more freely and more effectively than a young turtle.

Exercise Is Beneficial

In a pen that is set up with a lot of variety, your turtle will remain active and vital. You can encourage this with a couple of additional tricks.

Changing the Basking Spot: From observing your turtle, you know when it prefers to lie in the sun. Set up the pen in such a way that the turtle must find a different sunning place in the morning than in the afternoon because the shrubbery provides shade in different locations at different times. If these places are located opposite one another and with obstacles in between, your turtle will get some exercise in changing locations, especially if it has to swim or climb.

Dividing up the food: An exciting food search also stimulates the impulse to move. Large outdoor enclosures, in which every adult tortoise has around 100 square feet (12 sq m) of "pasture land" available, can be seeded with a special pasture and herb mixture for tortoises (from a pet shop). The various herbs grow throughout the year at different times and will even lure the turtle off well-worn paths by their smell. If the outdoor pen is significantly smaller, there is a danger that the herbs will be eaten too soon, along with their roots. You can reduce or prevent this overgrazing by feeding freshly cut greens every day.

Obstacles are often
surmounted directly. You can
keep the turtle physically fit by
positioning food and obstacles in the
right way.

Basking is an important feature
in a turtle's daily routine. It
provides the desired body
temperature and the beneficial
daily supply of UV rays.

**This alert Amboina Painted
Turtle** feels secure in shallow
water that also provides adequate
cover. This water allows the turtle to
survey its territory and drive away
intruders.

An adult turtle finds good cover
in the underbrush, as does
this Marginated Tortoise. A good
side effect is that the thick
vegetation also cleans the
creature's shell.

Random food dispensers hold the turtle's attention with astonishing effectiveness.

Fruit-producing plants in the enclosure: Berry bushes such as white, black, and red currants; raspberries; blackberries; and small juniper bushes produce ripe fruits right through the fall.

The fruits sometimes drop onto the ground in the enclosure. The turtle quickly learns that its daily search is rewarded with a surprisingly delicious result.

In addition, on hot summer days, the bushes provide variable shade into which your pet can withdraw. You can also feed clippings—the leafy branches—from blackberries.

Remove any fruits on the ground that your turtle has not eaten.

Treats in the Terrarium

In a partially shaded area inside the outdoor pen, you can set up a small compost pile for aquatic turtles that spend time on land (genera *Cuora* and *Chinemys*). Put a couple of rotten, untreated boards; small, old tree trunks; or thick branches at the foot of the pile.

Small creatures of all types will take up residence under the rotting wood. These include isopods, earthworms, grubs, bugs, and millipedes.

They eat the rotting plant material. The turtle will soon discover these tasty little creatures as it rummages around and will regularly go hunting for them.

If your pet is a species that practically never leaves the water, occasionally toss 1 or 2 of the collected food animals into the pond during the turtle's active time.

Installing a random food dispenser: With this dispenser, which you can easily install yourself, you perfect feeding on the randomness principle.

A plastic tube a little over 1 inch (3 cm) in diameter and 8 inches (20 cm) long is closed on both ends and has 5⁄32 inch (4 mm) holes 1 inch (2.5 cm) apart. Hang the tube over the water or the land so that the holes are on the bottom.

Put in 3 or 4 young crickets or creatures from the compost heap. As they scramble around, 1 or more bugs will fall out. This keeps the turtle alert, and lets it get some small treats.

Extending the Outdoor Time

The longer the turtle can spend in the outdoor enclosure, the better. In central latitudes in May and September, there are often nice, warm days that are still interrupted by cold periods. When in a greenhouse, the turtle can take advantage of the warm days during this time since it can pull back into the greenhouse when the weather gets cold.

That way, you make it possible for the turtle to spend 2 to 3 months longer outdoors with no adverse consequences. If you follow the suggested design for an aquatic turtle pond (see illustration on p. 45), you should use solar heating in this transitional time. It will make the pond usable for a longer time because the water is now warmer for the turtle.

MY PET

Have they gotten used to one another?

You have put another female in with your female tortoise. In an outdoor enclosure, you can observe the behavior of your pets particularly well. Is the living arrangement working out, or do the two quarrel?

The test begins:

Draw a sketch of your enclosure. Over a couple of days, mark down the trails used by the turtles. Note whether the rest areas are located away from one another. How often and for how long does one turtle disturb or pester the other? How often and for how long are meetings friendly? Do both turtles have a normal appetite? After a week or 10 days, if both creatures are at ease and are getting their share of the food, it is working.

My test results:

Handling Turtles Properly

Somebody gave us a large Slider, and we keep it in the yard. Now we want it to have a routine checkup, but even my husband is hesitant to pick up the feisty creature. My daughter insists on picking up the turtle herself. What is the best way to do this?

THERE ARE SOME SIMPLE RULES to observe when handling a turtle. These are based on defensive behavior, which depends on age and species.

Recognizing Defensive Behavior

Since a young turtle's shell is still too soft to provide effective protection, young turtles generally defend themselves by flailing violently with their limbs. However, adult turtles are very conscious of their fortress. In the presence of danger, they defend themselves by pulling in their head and limbs. Depending on how they react, there are two identifiable classes: the hidden-neck turtles and the side-neck turtles. The first group includes all tortoises plus many species of aquatic turtles. They all bury their head and neck inside their shell by pulling them in. The other group, to which many aquatic turtles belong, protect their head and sensitive, usually quite long neck by tucking them into a groove between the upper and lower shells. In so doing, they turn their neck toward the rear. This group includes the William's Mud Turtle, Snake-necked Turtle, Matamata, and Short-necked Turtle (all discussed in this book) plus a few other species.

The Right Way to Handle a Turtle

You now know your turtle's defensive behavior and can deal with it in the following way. Young hidden-neck turtles are picked up with the thumb and forefinger by grasping them from above on the sides, midway along the top shell, as if your hand were a set of tongs. Older, heavy turtles are grasped left and right on upper and lower shells with both hands along the sides. Pick up young side-neck turtles with thumb and index finger, as if they were tweezers, by the rear, so that the turtles cannot bite—which they will try to do, even though they are small. Adult animals are picked up in the same way as the young ones but with both hands. With heavy, aggressive turtles, wear work gloves as a precaution to protect yourself from getting bitten.

Practice Picking up a Turtle

Let your daughter calmly pick up the turtle—at first just a short distance off the ground. If she becomes frightened and drops the turtle, it will not get injured. That way, she will find out how much strength the turtle brings to its defensive behavior and will quickly adapt to it. Then she will soon be able to handle any turtle.

Taking Care of Multiple Turtles

You always hear people say that turtles need a partner in order to live out their social behavior. This is understandable for humans, who are social creatures. However, this human need is not so easily transferred to a turtle.

It is true that turtles show certain behavior patterns when they meet others of their kind, which they do not experience when they are alone. This applies especially to competitive behaviors, which the female may develop for a while before laying eggs.

It is also true that intraspecies communication, especially with a mate, leads to one of the most interesting behavior patterns that can be observed. In this instance, it is important to ensure the welfare of the mating pair so that neither partner is harmed. In other words, they must be under constant supervision.

So far, it has not been scientifically proven that your turtle will be missing something important in its life if it has no opportunities to meet other turtles.

A creature of the same sex: A female turtle that is put in with another female of its species experiences no vitally important change to its welfare. However, a harmonious coexistence can produce an intraspecies contact that is interesting to watch.

Turtles of the opposite sex: If you put a male in with a female, he will immediately try to court the female. In the wild, the female can get away if she finds the suitor too troublesome. Alternatively, the male can turn to a different female he meets along the way. In other words, the male in no way provides amusement for the female. In the long run, the encounters in the pen cannot be reduced to a reasonable amount. Male aquatic turtles are even notorious for tirelessly pestering their partners.

The Eastern ▶ Box Turtle *gets along well with others of its species in the enclosure. It likes shady, moist, warm hiding places.*

Interpreting Social Contacts Properly

Undesirable pursuit: Male tortoises are generally no less persistent than aquatic turtles. Now, one might conclude that the uninterrupted pursuit of a female is an elementary need on the part of the male, which must be allowed so that it can experience life as it was meant to.

tent flight and later on with apathy and a refusal to eat.

The pursuer often bites the other occupant until it bleeds. In the worst case, the latter may even die. Male Russian Tortoises and males of the *Cuora* species are notorious for this type of tireless and violent aggression. Even adolescent creatures, such as the Pancake Tortoise, occasionally display this behavior.

Do not subject your turtle to this behavior or judge the behavior to be

DID YOU KNOW THAT . . .

. . . turtles do not need the company of other turtles?

In a wolf pack or a prairie dog colony, every member profits from the social cohesion of the group. With wolves, hunting success increases. With the prairie dog, it is about security. In contrast, the turtle has chosen the life of a loner. Being alone makes a turtle less visible to a predator than if it were in a larger association. An assembly of tortoises is much easier for predators to find than an inconspicuous individual animal. Only the fast swimmers among the aquatic turtles have the luxury of forming an emergency community, when they occupy a basking place on one of the rare roots in the water. One of the sun worshipers always keeps an eye peeled. In the presence of danger, it alerts the others by fleeing into the water.

That conclusion would be completely wrong.

In the wild, a turtle has many more opportunities to get away. In the enclosure, the creature that is relentlessly pursued—which can also be a male rival—at first reacts with consis-

malicious. Aggression in the wild has a purpose. There it is not harmful, because every creature has the possibility of getting away. However, that is not the case inside your enclosure. That is why the responsibility falls to you to end it immediately.

Even when your turtle is resting, it is active.
It is observing its surroundings **with all its senses,**
testing scents, and feeling vibrations.

The Right Way to Put Turtles Together

Even though beginners should at first keep individual turtles, you should develop the courage to get involved in the adventure of breeding turtles as soon as you have adequate experience in caring for them. Reproduction is an important and very interesting part of your pet's behavior repertory.
With whom? You should put two creatures together in a sufficiently large enclosure for breeding purposes. You should put the turtle that appears to be dominant in with the subordinate one—generally the more aggressive male in with the female. The latter thus retains the home court advantage of the familiar surroundings and knows the escape routes.

This method is especially called for when the male immediately and vigorously gets down to business and the female needs a little more time to get used to the new suitor. Since you are placing the male into a strange territory with which it is not familiar, this could initially slow things down—maybe for only 10 seconds for this strategy does not always work.

Experienced breeders put the female in with the male. When that happens, the mating usually occurs more quickly and the turtles can be separated promptly.

Social Young Turtles

If you have succeeded in breeding your tortoises, then you will notice a behavior in the young that may impress you as being social. Specifically, many young tortoises lie close together in a hideout. Do not interpret this as a need for comrades; they are simply sharing a secure hiding place. As soon as they grow larger, they change their behavior and become confirmed loners.

A healthy young tortoise's shell is smooth and round.

▼

Turtle Reproduction

It is exciting to follow close up how turtles mate and
how the little ones hatch from the eggs. However, the youngsters
need your help to get started in life.

Breeding Turtles

The number of turtles in the wild has been decreasing for about 50 years.
The main reasons are habitat destruction and the capture of wild animals for consumption.
Breeding your own turtles helps reduce loss through animal trafficking.

IN ORDER TO PROTECT A THREATENED SPECIES from extinction, the most important measure is habitat protection. With turtles, breeding in captivity can also make a significant contribution to preservation, especially when it involves a species that was previously removed from the wild in large numbers for pet ownership. This practice threatens their survival in the wild, which is why many species are protected today.

Species Protection

Perhaps *species protection* means for you mainly that it is forbidden to catch protected animals in the wild. This is just one side of the legal stipulation.

It is also forbidden to release animals that are kept as pets into the wild—regardless whether they are indigenous or alien species.

Catastrophic effects: The example of the Red-eared Slider shows that this species threatens indigenous animal populations—not just in its original home range, the U.S., but also in Europe and Asia—wherever it is released. It crosses with other wild subspecies and forces less-hardy species out of their habitats.

In addition, it also successfully destroys the small animal life in the strange biotope with its ravenous hunger for spawn and young amphibians and fish, as well as mollusks and plants.

Legal Protection for Turtles

As a result of these dangers, which affect the entire animal world equally, species protection laws have been enacted. They regulate not only the possession and keeping of animals but also the breeding and transfer of the animals, regardless of whether you received them as a gift or in exchange

TIP

Protection of turtles and tortoises

In 2005, the U.S. Fish and Wildlife Service added 13 turtle species to Appendix III of the Convention on International Trade in Endangered Species of Wild Fauna and Flora. The list contains the Alligator Snapping Turtle *(Macroclemys terrinckii)* and 12 species of North American Map Turtles *(Graptemys spp.)*, whose numbers in the wild have been declining.

What Does Species Protection Require of Me?

You can find out information about your responsibilities as a pet owner by consulting turtle and tortoise clubs and by checking the Internet. If you use the Internet, double-check what you learn because not all information on the Internet is accurate or reliable.

○ Keep any and all papers that come with any pet turtle that you purchase.

If your turtle produces offspring,

○ Determine if the offspring are subject to any reporting requirements. If so, report them individually. You may be required to have a CITES document as an ID for each creature. At that point, you are free to pass on the young creatures to other owners. You are again possibly subject to reporting requirements.

For information on the protection status of your pet:

○ The list of protected species is continually updated. Online databases contain the current text of species protection legislation. Local and regional turtle and tortoise clubs may also be able to provide reliable information.

for money. Remember, you are in possession of the animals if you carry them around with you. You do not need to be their owner—their caregiver—to be in possession of them.

Protection status: Many tortoises and aquatic turtles are protected. You need to check whether your pet belongs to these species.

If you want to take care of a turtle from a protected species, first do some thorough investigating (e.g., online, with the U.S. Fish and Wildlife Service, with your state wildlife department, with a university extension service, and so on). You will need to determine if possession is lawful, and if so, whether there are any reporting or other requirements.

At point of purchase: As a beginner, you can play it safe by getting any relevant papers with your new turtle.

If no papers are available and you do not know the protection status, at least get the following information: name and address of the seller, both the turtle's English and taxonomic names, and information on the sex of the animal (if it can be determined).

If you get the young turtle from a breeder, also get its birth date and any information from breeding records and about the parents.

If your turtle is imported, it may be subject to special regulations.

The bottom line is that you should know the regulations that apply to your particular case. Following the rules will not only benefit you, but also society in general.

Follow regulations: Breeders and dealers can tell you the necessary steps for you to keep your pet legally. These regulations keep changing. So you must get current information before purchasing your turtle. The legislators prescribe the turtles' identifying features so that the animals can be positively identified. Large animals that weigh over 18 ounces (500 g) need to be marked with a microchip, also known as a transponder. A transponder is not necessary if the animal weighs less than 18 ounces (500 g) or cannot attain that weight. Photo documentation is also used with animals that weigh more than 18 ounces (500 g), because in the past, microchips kept getting lost or stopped functioning. The turtle is placed onto a grid to indicate size and photographed top and bottom. With young animals, this is done at regular intervals until they are grown. The local environmental protection authorities can provide further details in individual cases.

The CITES Document

A CITES certificate is required for transporting and marketing species contained in Appendix A of the Convention on International Trade of Endangered Species. This does not apply to species in Appendix B. A certificate is always needed for export. This also applies to creatures bred in captivity.

General Knowledge and Minimum Standards

An owner can transfer an Appendix B animal if the recipient has the required knowledge. Before an ownership permit is issued, the transporter can test your knowledge and inspect your enclosure. Standards for ownership are held in close compliance with regulations on environmental protection. You assure the turtle's survival by observing the minimum standards, under which no harm comes to the animal. The minimum standards for reptiles were developed in cooperation with experts from zoos and science consultants. The specifications in this book are higher than the minimum requirements, so your pet will surely be in good hands.

Once the female has scraped a hollow in the vegetation with her hind feet, she carefully slips her eggs into it. ▶

MY PET

How aggressive are your turtles?

Certain species are generally known for aggressiveness, which increases during the mating season. This aggressiveness is based on the need to possess a territory all for itself. Find out if your have potentially aggressive turtles.

The test begins:

It is assumed that the turtles are familiar with the enclosure and that you are always present. You can judge the degree of aggressiveness by how directly the animals approach one another. The aggressiveness is most pronounced when one animal storms after the other. The second turtle flees but still gets bitten whenever the pursuer catches up with it. The only hope of peaceful coexistence is if you can manage to get the animals together without any consequent ill effects.

My test results:

Courtship and Mating

If you have managed to put together a mating pair of turtles successfully, you can look forward to some exciting moments watching your pets. You will be captivated by the male's courtship tricks, especially if you have Sliders or Red-bellied Short-necked Turtles; their strategies are particularly varied.

Alternatively, you can follow the female in her industrious efforts to soak up as much sunshine as possible to help the eggs inside her body ripen, to dig out a hollow, and to bury her eggs inside the hollow.

Note: As you watch your animals, please remain very discreet. The turtles often interrupt their actions as soon as they notice you because they may want to beg for food.

Keeping several turtles or a pair for breeding is always a difficult task. Keeping them separated requires a lot of space, and a large outdoor enclosure is a plus when it comes to mating rituals.

Breeding associations are therefore a good alternative, especially if you have space limitations. You borrow the turtle partner only for the brief mating time and subsequently share the offspring.

Note: In contrast to tortoises, aquatic turtles mate most frequently in the water. There are exceptions, though. For instance, with terrestrial swamp turtle species, such as the Yellow-margined Box Turtle, mating takes place on land.

Getting Ready for Mating

Separating the partners: Keep the partners separated for 3 to 4 weeks before the first mating of the season by providing each one with its own enclosure or part of one. Large outdoor enclosures are exceptions. The trick to successful mating involves making one partner desirous of an encounter by keeping them separated temporarily.

Getting ready for winter is another good opportunity to separate animals that have been living together in the same enclosure. After the end of hibernation, mating usually occurs rather quickly.

The first meeting: After hibernation, generally in the spring, start by putting the two animals together in an enclosure. At first, keep them separated in two sections divided by a board. The turtles cannot see each other, but they can smell the other's presence. Often the mere scent of the other turtle is enough to make the animals restless. They may even try to climb over the partition separating them. Keep a constant watch over the animals once you remove the divider, for now comes the first meeting—and it is very exciting. Pay close attention to whether the turtles tolerate one another. If the initial contact goes smoothly, subsequent spot checks will let know if your turtles' manners are still acceptable. However, if the two partners do not get along right from the beginning, separate them immediately for their own safety.

The mating ▶
season for the
Marginated
Tortoise *begins as*
early as March,
both in the wild
and when kept in
a greenhouse.

Do not judge the courtship ritual of your turtle by **human standards.** The turtle ritual has been successful for millions of years.

Watching the Courtship Ritual

Tortoises: Most males are fairly patient suitors, who circle around their female as a prelude. By gently biting on the front legs and bumping with the shell, they finally persuade her to stop and pull in her head and front legs.

Sometimes even the females are surprisingly active and can really arouse a hesitant partner by physically attacking him. In the course of this happy togetherness, copulation suddenly occurs, during which many male tortoises emit clearly audible guttural sounds. If the female is not willing, she flees while the male, intent on mating, is still on the rear of the female. If the female cannot get away from the male, separate them.

Young turtles that you have bred in captivity are a good indication of your skill as an owner.
▼

Aquatic turtles: Male Sliders, Painted Turtles, and Red-bellied Short-necked Turtles are really artful deceivers. The standard program of their courting ritual includes trembling with the forelegs. Painted turtles also display a ritual head nodding. Short-necked Turtles attempt to beguile the partner by fanning with a foreleg and cuddling with the head. When the male's courtship ritual intensifies, the male swims behind the female and copulates with her. Male Mud Turtles, on the other hand, often get right down to business. They mate with their partner immediately and without any recognizable greeting formalities. Presumably this behavior is due to the low-visibility habitat in which one could quickly lose sight of a potential mate during an elaborate courtship.

After Successful Mating

Immediately after mating, aquatic turtles need to be put back into separate enclosures—or separate them after 2 to 4 days if the animals remain peaceable. With many tortoises, it is still a good idea to separate them immediately. The only time you could keep them together is if they are in a particularly large outdoor enclosure with several females and only one male. This way a single female will not be relentlessly pursued by the male. Until the eggs are laid, you can see if the partners show any renewed interest in one another by putting the turtles back together after a few days. That way several matings at intervals of a few days may occur, which increases the fertilization rate of the eggs. In the wild, a female copulates with a number of males.

Note: Females can store sperm in their fallopian tubes for up to 4 years (e.g., Diamondback Terrapins). They can thus fertilize several clutches before the eggshells are formed, even when no male is present.

encouraging egg maturation. This will be particularly noticeable with Mud and Musk Turtles. During this time, the females rarely tolerate competition for the egg-laying place and will defend it temporarily, but emphatically, from other females.

Choosing a nesting place: The female searches for a nesting place in the terrarium, usually around the edges of

DID YOU KNOW THAT . . .

. . . the temperature in the nest often determines whether hatchlings are male or female?

With many turtle species, the sex of the embryos is not determined by heredity. For example, with *Clemmys guttata*, sex is determined by the temperature of the eggs in the hollow. Depending on the species, the formative time can vary in length. It extends from the time the eggs are laid through the twentieth day of egg maturation. With the species that have so far been studied, females hatch at higher temperatures and males at lower ones.

Watching the Eggs Being Laid

Taking care of the female: After successful mating, make sure that the female remains well nourished. She will now need more calcium. After a couple of weeks, she should be able to search at leisure for a quiet place to lay her eggs.

Female aquatic turtles that otherwise have never been on land will now regularly be found in the sun on land, where they seek to keep their body temperature at the ideal level for

the heat lamp, where the surface reaches over 86°F (30°C).

As soon as the turtle walks about restlessly, tests the ground with its nose, starts to scrape depressions with the hind feet, and ceases to take in much food, you know that egg laying is imminent. On such days, it is worthwhile to keep an eye on the turtle in the dusk if you want to watch the eggs being laid (without being seen!). Soon the female will dig a hollow that is about half as deep as the length of her shell.

Clutch size: Depending on the species, some turtles lay just 1 egg per clutch, like the Pancake Tortoise. Others lay between 15 and 18 eggs, like the European Tortoises. The size of the clutch depends on the age of the female, its vitality, and its body size and shape. A turtle may lay eggs once or several times in a year. If a turtle produces several clutches per year, the eggs are laid in intervals of several days or weeks, depending on the species.

Digging up the eggs: You should not simply leave the eggs on their own— turtles do not brood. Rather, you should carefully dig them up from the nest without turning them. Use a soft pencil to write on the shell the date on which each egg was laid. In order to incubate the eggs artificially, you need an egg chamber to hold the eggs and an incubator for the egg chamber. The eggs develop inside until the young hatch. By the way, with turtles, it is usual to speak not of incubating the eggs but, rather, of maturing them, as the development of the eggs is correctly termed.

TIP

Avoiding condensation

Undesired condensation on the lid of the egg chamber forms only when the chamber is in an environment that is colder than the interior climate. So it is best if you put your homemade incubator into a Styrofoam box with a lid to keep condensation from forming.

Maturing Turtle Eggs

Place the eggs you have dug out of the nesting cavity into an incubator. You can buy one in a pet shop or put one together yourself. The success of the hatch depends solely on the vitality of the embryo and your care in creating the right climate inside the incubator.

A Homemade Egg Chamber

The egg chamber holds the eggs and assures adequate humidity. Use a transparent plastic container that you fill halfway with vermiculite or insulation from a building supplies store. Instead, you can use construction sand if necessary. Add water to a depth of just over $1/16$ inch (2 mm) to keep the insulation moist. Sink the eggs halfway into the substrate—topside facing up— and close the container with a well-fitting lid. The necessary humidity of 90 to 100 percent will now develop inside the container. Open it up once a day, and use the lid to fan fresh air into the egg chamber.

Make sure no condensation from the lid drips onto the eggs. They could die if they get too wet. So place the container with one side on a matchbox. The container will stand at an angle, and the condensation on the inside of the lid will run to the edge.

A Homemade Incubator

This provides the appropriate warmth for the egg chamber. It consists of a simple plastic aquarium in which you place two bricks standing on end. Then fill it with water to just below the upper edge of the brick. Bricks are heavy, but they store heat well. Now place the egg chamber onto the bricks. Heat the water with an aquarium heater so that the temperature in the chamber is 82°F (28°C). The temperature can vary by a couple of degrees but must never fall below 77°F (25°C) or exceed 86°F (30°C). Cover the aquarium with a pane of glass that you set at an angle by inserting a small wooden wedge so that any condensation on the underside of the pane can run off to the side.

An Emergency Incubator for all Cases

If you get surprised by a clutch of eggs, you can put together the following incubator quickly. Fill a flowerpot 80 percent full with moist, washed river sand from the nearest sandbox or a building supplies store. Bed the eggs in the sand, and cover it all over with a pane of glass. To facilitate draining condensation to the side, place a match between the glass and the top rim of the flowerpot. The glass is now at an angle and thus facilitates a certain amount of air exchange.

By pouring a little water into the saucer beneath the flowerpot, you maintain a slight moisture in the sand. That way, you keep the eggs from drying out and have enough time to put together a functioning incubator.

Is the Egg Fertilized?

Experienced terrarium enthusiasts can tell in the first few days with the soft-shelled, white eggs of many aquatic turtles if an egg is fertilized or not. They can do this because of the abdominal band. This is a light stripe, at first visible only as a dot, that slowly grows in length. With Sliders the band is less

obvious but still recognizable as a change in coloration on the upper side of the egg.

The Right Way to Mature Turtle Eggs

▶ 1 **A standard incubator** is light, well insulated, finely adjustable, technically reliable, and immediately available when needed. The egg chamber with the eggs is already inside this egg chamber.

▶ 2 **A temporary egg chamber** is useful if the turtle unexpectedly lays eggs. The flowerpot version keeps the eggs from drying out and the embryos from dying. Healthy eggs survive the waiting period until a standard incubator is available with no problem.

Checking the eggs: You can weigh the eggs and look through them against a light. Fertilized eggs gain weight, which can be determined using a postal scale and weighing the eggs every 2 weeks. Unfertilized eggs slowly dry out and thus become lighter.

When candling the eggs, hold each one (with the marking facing up) between your thumb and forefinger in front of a desk lamp or the like in such a way that you are not blinded by the light. The light will make the egg seem to glow from inside. With fertilized eggs, you can see blood vessels and, in later stages of development, an increasing darkening: the embryo's stomach! Unfertilized eggs show two varied light areas. Specifically, you will see a very light air bladder and a somewhat darker part consisting of the remains of the yolk, which slowly dries up.

Exercising patience: Never open an egg. The embryos of many species will experience a developmental delay in the form of an exceptionally long maturation. By opening an egg prematurely, you can endanger the embryo's life. If an egg is clearly spoiled (with a dead embryo), it splits open.

Hatching

You can tell that hatching is imminent when you see cracks in the eggshells. A healthy baby turtle can take 1 to 3 days to hatch. It stops the process repeatedly to gather strength. You must not help, especially because you could damage any remaining yolk. Afterward, the babies can spend a few more days in the incubator until the leftover yolk is completely gone—assuming, of course, that the egg chamber is large enough. You should take a new container, line it with paper towels, and put the baby turtles inside it. Then put this new container into the incubator. If a young turtle gets stuck in the egg and dies or dies partially developed, there is a 99.9 percent probability that the embryo was not sufficiently vital. This lack of vitality has more to do with the mother's nutrition and vitality than with the performance of your incubator.

Raising the Young Turtles

Keep freshly hatched babies and adolescents separated from the parents. The requirements, such as light conditions, temperature, and food, are similar to those of adult creatures. After hatching and after the disappearance of the yolk sac, if applicable, the young turtles need about a week before they begin to eat. At this time, metabolism switches from digesting the yolk sac to digesting solid food. With both tortoises and aquatic turtles, the young creatures should have an opportunity to bask in the sun. Take this into account when you establish the dimensions of the nursery. The nursery should be portable so you can put it onto the balcony or terrace when the sun is shining. To keep the nursery from getting too hot, cover at least one-third of it with a reed mat to provide some shade.

If you put the young turtles into an outdoor enclosure, it must be secured against birds. Make sure the turtles get some direct sunlight, for ultraviolet rays cannot penetrate glass (see the tip on p. 122).

The First Few Hours
at a Glance

The Time Is Ripe

What causes the embryo to hatch? The larger it grows, the more oxygen it needs. As soon as the eggshell ceases to let in enough oxygen for its needs, the embryo breaks the shell.

◀ A Timid Start

The embryo uses its egg tooth to cut the inner membrane of the egg and break open the shell. At first, it creates an opening through which it can breathe fresh air. Then it has to gather its strength.

◀ The Light of the World

With increasing strength, the young turtle uses its head to break off pieces of the eggshell. It thus produces space for stretching out its front legs. Some long recovery pauses are still necessary.

Brought to Life ▶

After the baby leaves the egg, you can see how the embryo was folded up inside the shell. The fold in the plastron straightens out after a few days. There may be some leftover yolk, but it will disintegrate.

▲ A Lengthy Hatch

The creature can take 3 days to get from the first opening in the shell to this stage. The duration depends on the thickness of the eggshell and the strength of the hatchling. A baby turtle rarely gets stuck inside an egg.

Raising Aquatic Turtles: You can raise your baby turtles together in an aquarium. Set this up the same way you do an enclosure for the adult turtles. You can also use the quarantine tank.

Hiding places: Young aquatic turtles are not yet territorial. They get along with one another. However, there must be no competitive situations. Since the little ones are very shy and are concerned with camouflage, offer them more hiding places than there are turtles. You can calmly tolerate a clustering of numerous turtles in a particularly coveted hiding place as long as the sharing of space does not result in any quarrels that produce injuries. The young turtles are particularly fond of floating islands. These islands not only provide good cover and shade the water but also amount to large hiding places under which the turtles can move around freely.

Feeding: In the first 4 to 8 weeks, the best food you can offer the young creatures is live water fleas, mosquito larvae, and young earthworms, which satisfy the babies' hunting instinct. Later on, you can slowly transition to the described diet in the form of frozen and freshly killed fishes. You will quickly see that there are both fast eaters with accelerated growth and stolid eaters with slow growth. The larger animals soon use their advantage in finding food and chase away the weaker ones. If you see this happening, you should divide the young creatures according to size and thus make it possible for every individual to get its due. Weight records will help you keep track. To differentiate among the young turtles, you can mark them on the shell with fingernail polish.

Feeding the young turtles is very demanding. You have to pay particular attention the calcium-phosphorus balance and provide a constant supply of calcium and sunlight (UV light). Otherwise, the youngsters will experience softening of the shell, which can result in incurable deformities.

While you have floating or live food in the water, turn the filter off so that the food does not get whisked away from in front of the turtles' noses.

Raising tortoises: You can raise the young tortoises in a terrarium set up according to the needs of their species. Simply follow the specifications for configuring enclosures described in the Profiles and Technical sections.

Hiding places: Young tortoises prefer to live in hiding and often close to one another. Since they are so small and easily become dehydrated, there must always be some deep hiding places with moist ground available. A 2- to 3-inch (6 to 8 cm) layer of loose soil from the garden or deciduous leaf litter works well.

With tortoises, the best way to prevent vitamin D_3 deficiency and

---

TIP

No UV light in the greenhouse

Glass, fairly old Plexiglas, and double-ribbed polycarbonate panels do not let through the necessary UVB portion of sunlight, so this radiation cannot have any effect under glass. For this reason, you should let true greenhouse residents enjoy 10 to 20 minutes of direct sunshine every day.

Right from the first day, sunbaths are vitally important in helping the young turtle grow up healthy.

rickets (softening of the bones) is to grow up in natural sunlight. Depending on the height of the sun, about 10 to 20 minutes under a clear sky will suffice to meet a young animal's need for vitamin D_3.

Feeding: Food must be available all day long. Its quality is crucial for healthy growth. As with aquatic turtles, you have to watch the calcium-phosphorus balance in the food and provide a constant supply of lime and UV light. The young of many species (including the Pancake Tortoise) ingest the droppings of the parents. Presumably, doing so enriches their intestinal flora with useful microorganisms that help digest fiber. Offer the young creatures some fresh droppings from the parents one time and see if they eat it. If not, remove the droppings.

Questions About
Raising Turtles

? **What are the advantages of breeding clubs?**

Turtles are kept singly principally because of a lack of space. Generally, this lack of space is the hardest problem to solve. The advantages of a breeding club is that your turtle can reproduce without your having to construct a larger enclosure and you can still raise young turtles. The rules for a breeding club are simple. Whoever has the better setup gets to care for the partner. This person is not responsible for any unforeseen damages, though, such as if the turtle should get sick or die while in that person's care. The young turtles are divided up in such a way that the owner of the female gets to choose first, the owner of the male gets to choose second, and so forth. Each person gets to choose the animals from the group. They can also divide up the eggs if the owners want to

mature them. Food costs for the guest turtle are compensated through the sharing of the young. If veterinary treatments are necessary during the arrangement, each person pays for his or her own animal.

? **What is the dumpling effect? Somebody warned me about this, because I have acquired a young animal that eats very well.**

This expression means that young animals can swell up like yeast dumplings if they are not cared for properly. If the food has too little fiber and too much protein, or if the enclosure is too dark and too warm, then the young turtles swell up like dumplings. Unfortunately, the growth of the shell cannot keep up. It becomes soft, sinks in, or becomes hunchbacked. The process speeds up further if the young are allowed to continue hibernating and fattening up. So make

absolutely sure you stick to the information on proper nutrition and hibernation for young animals.

? **Just how quickly should my turtle grow?**

Healthy growth begins quite quickly in the first year and then decreases from year to year. Many species continue growing even in old age. Others, such as the *Terrapene* species, stop growing two years after reaching sexual maturity. You can use a series of measurements to tell if your turtle is growing within the normal range. In the first year, the lower shell of the *Terrapene* species increases in length by around 70 percent, by 30 percent in the second year, and by 20 percent in the third. These values can vary on the high or low side as long as the shell remains firm and free of distortion, the animal is lively, and pulling in the limbs does not produce any bulges of

fat. Another consideration is that the females of many species grow faster and larger than the males (see size specifications in "Profiles," pp. 22–31).

? Help! I cannot deal with the plethora of regulations on ownership and trade. What is the current story?

To begin with, you will find all laws and their applications arranged for an overview in the WISIA database maintained by the Division of Natural Preservation. I will mention briefly the regulations and laws that you can consult for your purposes.

—BArtSchV.: The National Species Protection Decree is interpreted by the environmental authorities of your area. It regulates the registration of turtles subject to reporting and keeps information about the purchase, sale, transfer, and death of young turtles.

—EU Law: Inside the member countries, this regulates dealing with protected species. Appendix A lists species with the highest protections status. Further categories in decreasing sequence are Appendices B, C, and D.

—CITES: An abbreviation for Convention on International Trade in Endangered Species of Wild Fauna and Flora. This international accord regulates worldwide transport of protected species outside the EU. Depending on the protection status, the regulations are observed more or less strictly. A species protected in CITES Appendix I enjoys the highest protection status. Species that are listed in Appendices II and III are subject to less-strict regulations.

? I encountered the following in the "price list of a breeder: Thb, 1.0 juv." What is the meaning of all this?

This "secret language" spares everyone in the know from long explanations. The first is the abbreviation for the Boettger's Tortoise, *Testudo hermanni boettgeri* (Thb). There are also abbreviations for some of the other common species (Thh: *T. hermanni hermanni*; Tm: *Testudo marginata*; Tg: *Testudo graeca*; Th: *Testudo horsfieldii*). The numbers mean the following: 1.0 = male; 0.1 = female; 0.0.1 = a young animal of undetermined sex; 1.1.3 = a mating pair with three young. The abbreviation juv. = juvenile, not yet sexually mature. It is used in abbreviated form in animal lists.

What to Do When Problems Arise

Most problems in caring for turtles are the result of mistakes. The better you know your turtle's behavior, the easier it is to avoid these errors.

Correcting Problems with Living Conditions

If you take good care of your turtle, your pet should feel perfectly fine in your care. Still, problems may arise that you have to solve quickly to keep the creature from getting sick. It is best not to let things get to that stage.

IT IS BEST TO AVOID the following problems by carefully applying the recommendations in this book.

The Enclosure Is too Cold

This can happen if the spotlight is not present or is removed. A draft can also produce unhealthy cold. If the temperature is too low, the turtle cannot achieve its preferred temperature for days or weeks. There is then a danger of the body's enzymes breaking down so that the food can no longer be digested and, instead, rots in the intestine. The immune system grows weaker, and the creature becomes susceptible to infections. Damage from cold often includes diarrhea, lung inflammation, swollen eyelids (Harder's glands), or an ear infection.

My tip: The turtle must be able to achieve its preferred temperature at least once a day. So check the temperature every day.

The Enclosure Is too Warm

Perhaps the terrarium is placed right in the sun or the cover keeps built-up solar heat from escaping. Your tortoise will at first try to get out of the enclosure. If it does not, succeed, it will dig in and lie there apathetically. It may instead stay in the water all day. If things get too warm in the water for an aquatic turtle, it comes out to try to cool off on land. Heat stress weakens the immune system, and the animal can become seriously ill. If your turtle displays one of the mentioned behaviors, you must immediately check the temperature.

My tip: Never set up the enclosure in such a way that it is subjected to direct sun. If necessary, check the temperature several times a day.

Practical armor: ▶
this is how well
an adult turtle
can protect itself
by pulling into
its shell.

◄ *If your tortoise keeps moving back and forth next to the glass, the microclimate in the terrarium may be at fault. Check it carefully.*

Lighting Problems

Protracted basking: Your turtle spends a lot of time lying under the spotlight. First check if the enclosure is too cold or if your turtle is helping egg development through additional warmth. If you can rule out these two instances, the behavior points to illness—especially if the creature appears apathetic when you pick it up. Take it to the veterinarian immediately.

My tip: A healthy animal seeks the spotlight or direct sunlight only temporarily to reach the desired optimal temperature in its body. Body temperature decreases slowly after leaving the area of the spotlight, but it is restored by more basking.

How much UV light is beneficial? An excess of UV light can be harmful to your turtle. The UVB rays, which are only a portion of the UV light, are responsible for the organism's health. As with humans, UV light is responsible for the formation of vitamin D_3 in the skin of turtles. If too little vitamin D_3 is produced, no calcium gets deposited in the skeleton. The shell can become soft, and the creature will develop with rickets.

A few years ago, an expert named Bernd Hoppe calculated that a turtle that lies under a 300-watt UV lamp with outstretched limbs for 6 minutes can form enough vitamin D_3 for an entire day. The lamp was hung 10 inches (25 cm) above the animal. The intensity of the lamp corresponded to a summer day. The temperature remained tolerable for the turtle. I have taken these calculations into account in my specifications in this book. With the recommended distance of 24 to 32 inches (60 to 80 cm) between the UV lamp and the turtle, the daily light exposure is 10 to 20 minutes. This is adequate and has worked out very well in practice. If the exposure is longer than this, an excess of vitamin D_3 is produced. However, the initial vitamin produced is broken down or decays under the influence of further UV radiation. UV light also functions under water, and this is significant for aquatic turtles. Fifty percent of the UV light that hits the surface of clear water still reaches a turtle swimming 8 inches (20 cm) below.

My tip: Replace UV light with either the sun or a spotlight but not with vitamin D_3 drops. These are not an adequate substitution. In addition, you could poison your pet with an overdose.

Restless Wandering or Swimming Around

If you have one animal: You have already ruled out the possibility that your turtle is suffering from egg binding and have checked that the temperature in the enclosure is correct. There is also no other animal in the terrarium or in the vicinity. Then one of the following factors could be responsible for the restlessness: draft, vibrations from machines or stereos, and strong odors, such as smoke from a fireplace or tobacco.

My tip: If you have determined one of the factors to be the cause for your pet's restless behavior, you should move the enclosure to an appropriate location if the disturbance continues unabated.

If you have two animals: Both turtles are living in the same enclosure. By running along the glass, one of them gives you the impression that it wants to get out. Instead perhaps it hides, becomes listless, and stops eating. Apparently, your pets are not getting

along with one another. Perhaps you did not see the initial persecution. However, now a mere glance from the dominant animal is enough to terrify the subordinate one. You know how this works if you have ever walked to the

Avoiding Illness

▶ 1 **An aquarium heater** helps—in addition to the filter heater—in keeping the water up to temperature. The protective cage keeps the turtle from getting burned on the heating element.

▶ 2 **A dark hideout** provides young turtles with safety and security. If this type of hiding place is always near, the turtle can be much more relaxed.

▶ **1** **A turtle on its back** can right itself again. It just needs a fulcrum to push against with one leg.

▶ **2** **It pushes against the fulcrum,** such as this tree stump, turns itself over, and lands on all fours.

▶ **3** **As this sequence shows,** the strenuous righting from lying on the back is usually quickly forgotten. However, if no fulcrum is available, the turtle's attempts to right itself can lead to fatal exhaustion.

other side of the street to avoid a person you simply could not stand!

You need to separate the turtles so that they can neither see nor smell one another. You will soon see that your depressed turtle will rediscover its former joy in life.

My tip: A glance can kill, in the truest sense of the word, if the subordinate turtle has no means of escape. Therefore, you must eliminate the possibility of visual contact.

Eliminating Sources of Danger in the Home . . .

. . . for aquatic turtles:

▶ The creatures can get caught on accessories, such as roots and stones under the water, and drown. Take this into consideration as you set up the turtle's enclosure.

▶ If the water level is not at least equal to the width of the shell, the turtle cannot right itself if it ends up on its back. It will drown.

▶ Unprotected heating elements can produce severe burns if young turtles go too near them to sleep.

▶ Substrate consisting of gravel with pebbles measuring about $\frac{1}{8}$ to $\frac{3}{16}$ inch (3 to 5 mm) for keeping fish in an aquarium often get eaten by turtles. The reason for this is not always clear. It often happens because the animal is suffering from a mineral deficiency. Another reason might be the use of grindstones in the stomach to help with digestion. Since many aquatic turtles have died from overloading their innards with gravel, you should not use this as a substrate.

. . . for tortoises:

▶ They can burn themselves on low-hanging spotlights.

▶ They may become wedged or buried under a heavy, unstable stone structure in the scenery.

▶ As with aquatic turtles, there is a danger to tortoises from eating sand in the terrarium. The creatures can die if their digestive tract becomes

plugged with sand. Tortoises that ingest excessive substrate are usually suffering from a mineral deficiency. On the other hand, there is no negative effect from occasionally eating dirt because of its loose, organic composition.

Eliminating Sources of Danger in the Outdoor Enclosure

▶ Young turtles can fall prey to birds, and to martens (weasels) or cats during the night. It is best to surround the enclosure with a 3-foot (1 m) fence and cover it with a protective net.
▶ If the outdoor enclosure and your yard are not totally secure, the turtle may get away.
▶ A sand or loam substrate in the outdoor enclosure harbors the danger that the turtle will eat pieces of it and plug up its digestive tract. It is important that plenty of food containing minerals is available inside the outdoor enclosure so that the turtle can meet its need.

My tip: Adhere to the specifications in this book when you set up the outdoor enclosure. That way, nothing can go wrong. Turtles may also occasionally ingest dirt when they grab food. There is no harm in this. However, if this happens intentionally and in significant amounts, you must consult a veterinarian.

TIP

Predicting behavior

Evaluate your European Tortoise's behavior also with respect to the season. Up until summer, the most active phases increasingly shift to the early morning and late afternoon hours. Make notes for yourself throughout the year. That way, you will be able to predict the turtle's normal behavior.

MY PET

Does my turtle use the UV lamp?

The best UV lighting serves no purpose if your turtle does not spend any time under it. So use this experiment to find out how long it takes your turtle to come and lie under the spotlight after you turn it on.

The test begins:

Write down the time you turn on the UV lamp and how long it takes your turtle to take a position under the spotlight. Usually, this should take only a couple of minutes. However, if it takes your turtle about a quarter-hour, then keep the lamp on longer so that the creature has a total of 10 or 15 minutes to enjoy the UV lighting. If you have several animals, see if they all have an adequate chance to use the lamp.

My test results:

If Your Turtle Escapes from the Outdoor Enclosure

To varying degrees, aquatic turtles and tortoises are capable of climbing over mesh wire fences and digging under fairly substantial barriers. There may be many reasons for this—such as a pond temperature that is continually too low, an unacceptable amount of food, or great psychological pressure from a dominant turtle. In these instances, your pet just wants to get away. However, I believe that the main causes for turtle escapes are pure curiosity, a desire to enlarge the territory, and a defective barrier that is easy for the animal to get over.

If the barrier is defective, you have a very good chance of finding your turtle again, for it is very strongly connected to its primary home. That is where it feels secure and gets its food. Since it gets its bearings from the position of the sun and landmarks encountered during its travels, it will usually find its way back with their help. Remember that a tortoise's territory in the wild, where it travels in search of food, can easily amount to 2½ acres (1 ha). The escape could become a problem if the turtle cannot find its escape hatch again and keeps looking for it around the enclosure or the fence. If it gets dark in the meantime, the turtle will bed down for the night. Then, after the sun goes down, you have your best chance of finding your pet.

My tip: If used from the outset, an opaque fence of adequate height installed on a foundation is an effective measure for preventing escapes.

If Your Turtle Becomes Withdrawn

If you can rule out an unfavorable climate in the enclosure as a cause for the behavior, you should check the following three possibilities.

Sensitivity to the weather: Your turtle pulls back into a hiding place on cloudy, cold days and does not even want to go to the feeding place. It is out of sorts because of the weather. It will be back on its feet once the weather turns sunny and warm again.

My tip: Help the turtle by leaving the spotlight on longer or temporarily increase the light's intensity.

Summer rest: In particularly hot summer months, species from the steppe regions, such as the Russian Tortoise, dig long tunnels in the ground into which they retreat. This is how they get through the dry season in the wild, when not much food is available. During this summer rest, the creatures take in no food.

Depending on the weather, animals that also hibernate may be active for only 3 months of the year. They go from summer rest right into hibernation and practically sleep straight through.

Other species that likewise rest in the summer include the Pancake Tortoise, the Mud Turtle, and the African Helmeted Turtle.

Hibernation: Generally, turtle species from temperate latitudes begin hibernation in October or November. Since this is genetically programmed, you must not interrupt this rhythm.

When a turtle ▶ scrapes a hollow with its front legs, it is looking for a hiding place in the dirt.

My tip: Both adult and young turtles must be readied for the winter. Only young animals that hatch in October can be coddled for 3 to 4 months before going into an abbreviated hibernation.

When the Turtle Grows Old

Your turtle can stay with you for the length of a human life. European Tortoises and the females of many aquatic turtles—such as Spotted Turtles—are known to have lived to the age of 120. The males of these extremely long-lived females live to "only" about 60 years, and many Sliders live to be a little older than 30.

The specifications are merely isolated experiences. New records are continually reported, naturally involving turtles in captivity. In the wild, a turtle may live to half the ages cited because of diseases or influences from human settlement, alterations to the landscape, and road construction.

How Is Old Age Manifested? An old turtle experiences no further measurable growth. It also loses the bright colors of youth. The skin and shell turn a single color and often very dark, which is known scientifically as age-related melanism.

However, a turtle will retain its vitality into old age. I have heard of female tortoises that continued to lay eggs at over 60 years of age.

The Turtle Dies

If the turtle dies, it is a sad event for your child. This will call for an appropriate mourning ceremony, which you as parents surely will support unconditionally. If you have a yard, presumably you will bury the creature there. You can also look for an appropriate site in a forest. You will merely want to keep the burial away from sources of drinking water and bury the turtle at least 20 inches (50 cm) deep.

If your child is older and wants to know the cause of death, you can offer the turtle to the veterinary medicine department of a university. It will provide a diagnosis of the cause of death, which may offer conclusions about faulty living conditions.

◀ *At least 20 years separate this cute youngster from his stately adult counterpart.*

Information on the Internet

With its search engines, the Internet is a productive source of information about turtles. When you enter a key word, you often get hundreds of articles on the relevant theme. So how do you get the best overview?

You can find informative, factual web sites with the latest scientific knowledge among the recognized national and regional turtle organizations. You will also find exciting links to museums, university science departments, and research centers that deal with turtles. Even private home pages contain some neat syntheses of scientific information.

A hundred years ago, the lecture halls of universities witnessed debates that were anything but factual. Sometimes this happens today on Internet forums, when "crusaders" go after one another. To avoid this, you should proceed using the rules in the checklist at the right. They are not always easy. However, by following them, you can contribute to an orderly, factual discussion in a forum.

CHECKLIST

Help on the Internet

An article can be founded in fact but may also be nothing more than an assumption. It is simple to tell the difference if you use the following test:

○ Get confirmation for statements on web sites by comparing the information with national turtle organizations or professional literature. You can tell good web sites and discussion forums by their style and tone.

○ A good, professional style always involves supporting one's statements with figures, descriptions of experiments, and one's own experience or other appropriate proofs, such as photos or the name of the article, book, or web site from which a statement was quoted. That way everyone can read it.

○ In differences of opinion, facts are given in support rather than attacking another person. One may also attempt to win you over to a different point of view.

○ It is still possible to work creatively with an unsubstantiated statement. As a precautionary measure, it is termed a "working hypothesis" and presented as such for discussion.

Pet Sitter's Guide

When you go away for vacation, a pet sitter will take care of your animal. Here you can write down everything that your substitute needs to know. That way, your turtle will get the best care and you can enjoy your vacation to the fullest. This guide can also serve well if you ever are sick.

My turtle's name is:

My turtle is from the following species:

This is its typical behavior:

Things it likes to eat:

This much every day:

This much X number of times per week:

In-between snacks:

The proper feeding times:

The food is kept here:

Housekeeping:

To be cleaned every day:

To be cleaned every week:

Things that help the turtle feel well:

Things to check every day:

What the turtle does not like:

Things my turtle must not have:

Other important items:

How to contact the vet:

My vacation address and phone:

INDEX

Page numbers in **bold print** refer to illustrations.

U

V

W

Y

ASSOCIATIONS AND CLUBS

California Turtle and Tortoise Club
560 Robinson Ave.
El Cajon, CA 92020
www.tortoise.org (web site has audio files of tortoise calls!)

Chicago Turtle Club
c/o Lisa Koester
6125 N. Fairfield Ave.
Chicago, IL 60659
chicagoturtle@geocities.com

New York Turtle and Tortoise Society
P.O. Box 878
Orange, NJ 07051-0878
QandA@nytts.org

Rio Grande Turtle and Tortoise Club
P.O. Box 20836
Albuquerque, NM 87154-0836
info@rgttc.org

Seattle Turtle and Tortoise Club
1135 11th Pl. S.W.
North Bend, WA 90845
turtleclubseattle@yahoo.com
(425) 281-7607

SOME HELPFUL BOOKS

Bartlett, R. D. and Patricia Bartlett. *Aquatic Turtles: Sliders, Cooters, Painted, and Map Turtles.* Hauppauge, NY: Barron's Educational Series, Inc., 2003.

———. *Box Turtles: Facts and Advice on Care and Breeding.* Hauppauge, NY: Barron's Educational Series, Inc., 2001.

———. *Turtles and Tortoises—Complete Pet Owner's Manual.* Hauppauge, NY: Barron's Educational Series, Inc., 2006.

Cook, Tess. *Box Turtles— Complete Herp Care.* Neptune City, NJ: TFH Publications, Inc., 2004.

Cursen, Sarah. *Those Terrific Turtles.* Sarasota, FL: Pineapple Press, 2006.

Kirkpatrick, David. *Aquatic Turtles—Complete Herp Care.* Neptune City, NJ: TFH Publications, Inc., 2006.

Palika, Liz. *Turtles and Tortoises for Dummies.* NY: Hungry Minds, Inc., 2001.

Patterson, Jordan. *The Guide to Owning a Box Turtle.* Neptune City, NJ: TFH Publications, Inc., 2004.

Wilke, Hartmut. *Tortoises and Box Turtles.* Hauppauge, NY: Barron's Educational Series, Inc., 2000.

———. *Turtles—A Complete Pet Owner's Manual.* Hauppauge, NY: Barron's Educational Series, Inc., 2006.

WEB SITES

www.geocities.com/heartland/village/7666/ The Chicago Turtle Club—for help in maintaining the well-being, safety, and environment of turtles and tortoises

www.matts-turtles.org. The Mid-Atlantic Turtle and Tortoise Society

http://members.aol.com/WAL-DIAL/ottslnks.htm Multiple links of interest to turtle and tortoise fans

www.nytts.org. The New York Turtle and Tortoise Society

www.reptilechannel.com/turtles-and-tortoises/default.aspx

www.sdturtle.org. The San Diego Turtle and Tortoise Society

www.tortoise.org The California Turtle and Tortoise Club

www.boxturtlesite.info The place to learn about box turtles.

MAGAZINES

EMYS, The International Journal of Turtle and Tortoise Husbandry; *http//zoomed.com/ecom/BrowseStore.php?category=26*

Herp Digest (free electronic magazine) *www.herpdigest.org*

Tortuga Gazette http://www.tortoise.org/tortugagazette.html

Answers to Questions on the Terrarium Hobby

Consult with your vet or a regional turtle and tortoise club. Some of the web sites listed above invite interested parties to submit questions.

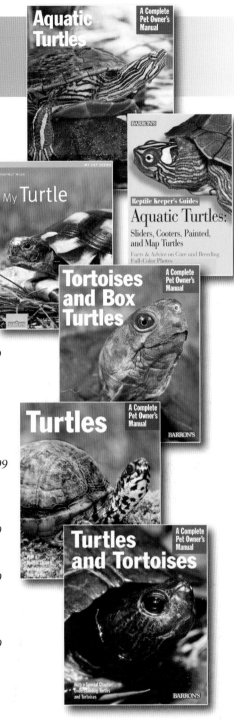

About the Author

Dr. Hartmut Wilke is a biologist. As director of the Exotarium of the Frankfurt Zoo (Germany) and of the Darmstadt Zoo (Germany), he has accumulated practical experience with turtles throughout his career. He regularly provides advice to turtle enthusiasts.

About the Photographer

Christine Steimer works as a freelance photographer and specializes in pet photography. She works for international book publishers, scientific periodicals, and advertising agencies.

Acknowledgment

The publisher and author are deeply grateful to Renate Keil, D.V.M. for the descriptions of diseases on pp. 93–97.

First edition translated by Eric A. Bye.

English translation © Copyright 2009 by Barron's Educational Series, Inc.

Original title of the book in German is *Mein Schildkröte.*

© Copyright 2007 by Gräfe and Unvzer Verlag, GmbH, Munich.

GU

All inquiries should be addressed to:
Barron's Educational Series, Inc.
250 Wireless Boulevard
Hauppauge, New York 11788
www.barronseduc.com

Library of Congress Catalog Card No. 2008044356

ISBN: 978-0-7641-4192-8

Library of Congress Cataloging-in-Publication Data
Wilke, Hartmut, 1943–
 [Meine Schildkröte. English]
 My turtle / Hartmut Wilke. — 1st ed.
  p. cm.
 Includes bibliographical references and index.
 ISBN-13: 978-0-7641-4192-8
 ISBN-10: 0-7641-4192-9
 Turtles as pets. I. Title

F459.T8W4913 2009
639.3'92—dc22   2008044356

Printed in China
9 8 7 6 5

Photo Credits

Christine Steimer, except for Uwe Anders (p. 26, bottom and p. 28, top).

Cover Photos

Christine Steimer.

Important Note

If you are scratched or bitten by your turtle, you should consult a physician immediately.

The electric equipment described in this book for use with terrariums must be of UL-listed design and construction. Keep in mind the hazards associated with the use of such electric appliances and wiring, especially near water. The use of an electronic circuit breaker that will interrupt the flow of electricity if damage occurs to appliances or wiring is strongly recommended. A protective switch, which must be installed by a licensed electrician, serves the same purpose.